EXTRAORDINARY
TENNIS
FOR THE
ORDINARY PLAYER

EXTRAORDINARY TENNIS FOR THE ORDINARY PLAYER

WINNING STRATEGY FOR THE TENNIS ENTHUSIAST WHO PLAYS FOR FUN

by

Simon Ramo, Ph.D.

CROWN PUBLISHERS, INC.   NEW YORK

Second Printing, May, 1970

© 1970 by Simon Ramo
Library of Congress Catalog Card Number: 75–101594
Printed in the United States of America
Published simultaneously in Canada by
General Publishing Company Limited

Design by Christine Schacker

Dedication

To the many tireless and a greater number of tired mediocre tennis players whom I have observed and analyzed; who regularly perform miracles in the synthesis of misconceptions, mistimings, and mistakes into opportunities for their opponents, which these equally inept nonathletes almost always fail to exploit; without whose endless production of pertinent, creative, and discouraging data this book could not have been written

Contents

"No gentleman should be too good at a sport"—old English saying.

Preface

I ALWAYS KNEW myself to be—and destined never to be more than—an "ordinary" tennis player; "mediocre" would be more accurate. If, as is usually claimed, it is beneficial to play with players who are better than you are, then I could also be categorized as the most highly benefited player I know. Yet, somewhere along the line, it began to occur to me that those peculiar combinations of circumstances that caused me to win a point occasionally were not necessarily correctly regarded as accidents. Or, put more substantively, if they were accidents, I really had it in my power to cause them to happen more often, rather than so seldom—and my opponents, assuming an equal interest in the matter, could have done some things to prevent these accidents.

Let me hasten to say that I have discovered no magic to enable a clumsy, slow, uncoordinated, dim-witted novice to embarrass a polished tennis specialist, an unusual athlete in top form. But I am not that bad, nor are the tennis regulars or irregulars I play with that good. Allowing for variations of speed, power, age, and coordination, we are all properly listed as average players, give or take an exceptionally big serve here, a bad knee there, a six-weeks layoff to go to Europe, a young son suddenly arriving as a doubles partner

9

right off the junior college tennis team, or a girl with a surprisingly accurate and strong backhand. Put aside the champions and the near-champions, the natural athletes who put everyone else to shame at any sport, and there are left the rest of us—by the thousands—ordinary and sometimes even much above average, who enjoy tennis and especially enjoy winning at it, who can individually make much more use of our ability (and win-ability) by adjusting our ideas of what we should be up to on the court.

If the full potential of the average player is to be approached, the mental component of his tennis should be raised up to the competence level of the physical aspects of his play. But who wants to do analytical homework before a game, and trot onto the court loaded with memorized formulas and bulging with a microminiaturized computer in his shirt? Fortunately, there is an easier route to becoming an "ex-ordinary" tennis player. It all starts with dropping some patterns of thought and consequent action. To put it bluntly, we have all been overly impressed and influenced by the way the top players, the pros and champions, play tennis and write about playing tennis. We think that *their* game is *the* game; that the closer we can get to a full imitation of their motions and strategy, the more points we shall win. Not so. Some things they do we should emulate (like the way they dress), but most of our exaggerated and determined mimicry of the unexcelled, top-seeded tennis stars does us in. We should forsake this aspirational Everest and proceed toward our own suitable peaks at our own comfortable pace.

As tennis players, we are, to use an analogy, middle class or upper middle class, or maybe even affluent, in our resources and endowments, but we are not "rich as Rockefeller." To continually overcommit these resources achieves more dire consequences than occasional self-overkills; it leads to losing. Avoiding this and substituting for it a winning approach is what this book is about.

EXTRAORDINARY
TENNIS
FOR THE
ORDINARY PLAYER

1

Two Different Games, One Name

PEOPLE WHO PLAY tennis think there is only one game called "tennis." Actually there are two, and I am not referring to clay courts or grass courts. These separate games, which happen to be passing under the same name, use identical instruments—that is, balls and rackets. They are played on the same courts, and they rely on the same scoring and rules. Expressions such as "six-four," "set-point," "deuce," and "love" are heard equally often around both kinds of encounters. But the two games are really very different.

The reason why it is worth recognizing that there are two games and not just one is that most tennis players have no business playing one of them. They cannot do it well, and they lose some of their happiness by trying. But it is worse than this. What they actually do is play one game while thinking they are playing the other. It is like being a cat and thinking you are a dog. This is not good because you get along rather poorly with dogs, and you don't do too well with cats either. If you are a cat you ought to know that you are a cat and learn to exploit living as a cat.

Now, some people can enjoy very much playing one of the two games of tennis, and other people can be exhilarated by the other one. Whichever group you belong in, you will enjoy tennis more if, at the least, you play the game that you understand yourself to be playing, rather than engaging in one game under the mistaken assumption that you are involved in the other.

Let me illustrate. Assume that two games, one of each kind, are taking place side by side on adjacent courts. At this point, for reasons that will become apparent in a moment, we shall start calling the two games by names that are close to being useful descriptions. The first we shall name "pro tennis," which does not mean that the two players who are playing it are professionals, although they may be. The other tennis game, on the adjacent court, we shall label "ordinary" tennis, which does not say that the players are necessarily terrible or inexperienced, awkward, slow, sloppy, incapable of hitting a backhand or getting anything but a gentle, high floating serve in. It just means, as the dictionary suggests, that they are undistinguished, of average capacity, a little dull to watch, more commonplace than inspired. Now let us observe these two games in progress.

The pro-tennis encounter is a singles match. Both players have a very hard serve, the first serve even faster than the second. The first one is virtually impossible to return well, and is often an ace (untouched) when it goes in, which it does much of the time. The second serve is easier to return, but still quite difficult. We observe that the server always rushes toward the net after his serve. The receiver, if he gets his racket on the serve, usually finds that he can only hit the ball up, for what is quite often a put-away by the server. Sometimes, however, the receiver hits a good return shot that passes the server and scores on him. The better of the two players does this more frequently and, moreover, when he does not succeed in passing the server, he at least gets a good low ball back, which the server then is often forced to offer up for the receiver to smash with a well-placed volley.

Occasionally, though rarely, the two actually get themselves into a competitive situation at the back lines, with each hitting very hard drives toward the corners. These bounce in just barely, but nevertheless safely so, each player forcing the receiver of the ball to the maximum of speed and agility to return it.

Almost always the point is scored when one of the two gets a really good crack at a ball and hits it so well placed away from his opponent, and (or) so hard, that the recovery is impossible. We observe that these two players have what looks to a casual observer to be equally strong forehands and backhands. They can hit the ball running forward, backward, or sideways. They can pick it up off the ground, with or without a bounce, depending upon what the situation requires. They can run back on a high one and come through with an overhead smash as the climax of the process.

The pro-tennis players warm up for many minutes before starting their game. During the warm-up period, each of them takes his turn at the net and hits a large number of well-placed balls backhand and forehand with good speed and control, before he is willing to start the play.

A warm-up in the court where the "ordinary" game is carried on is practically nonexistent. There is much talk, particularly between women, with many balls going directly into the net from the first, start-off bounce. Any ball directed within reasonable proximity of the opposing warmer-upper will be hit at casually—and often returned completely out of range of the opponent, or out of the court. After eight or ten such attempts, with, granted, a few well-hit balls on a good day, two or three or all four of the players become impatient with and bored by the chasing of balls, which is what their warm-up largely consists of—or perhaps with the subject matter under discussion.

At this point someone suggests that they start. It's "first one in" for each server. If the first ball is indeed put in, then no matter how punk a serve it is and how easy to return, the receiver is quite likely to hit it into the net or send it past the back base line, being completely unprepared. The first few games, in fact, are actually a warm-up period that sets a standard for the erraticism maintained for much of the match.

Focusing now on the individual players on the court where the ordinary tennis game is taking place, let us go a step further and assume that though these four players vary, they share mediocrity. I said four because, of course, they are playing doubles—a mediocre singles tennis game is too pitiful to watch, and we wouldn't think of doing it. We'll start with Wilhelm, age thirty-seven, the best of the four players. He was on his college tennis team for one year. He is a good athlete, with natural form, speed, and timing. He had good tennis instruction in his youth and knows tennis well—pro tennis, that is—the kind of tennis taught by the teachers, written up in the books, and played by the professionals.

The only thing is, Wilhelm's work requires that he do a lot of traveling. Also, he has to play golf for social-sales purposes, even though he much prefers tennis. So he has lost contact with his fellow pro-tennis players. He finds himself in mixed doubles about once every three weeks in the summer with his wife. He never gets a half-hour of hitting balls back and forth with a good player.

Wilhelm's first serve is very hard. It is an "in" serve about one in ten or twenty times. When he was younger and playing often, it used to go in once every three or four times, and was rarely returned. When it goes in now, it is rarely returned. But these days it is usually a fault, and that puts him under pressure to be sure to get his second serve in. It is kind of embarrassing to have the second serve also a fault, especially if he is behind in the scoring. A double fault distresses him *and* his wife. So, the way he plays his games now is by easing up on his second one considerably as the game progresses. He commences to look a little bit awkward and gets overly careful. This helps him to double quite often. The first time he doubles, both he and the others blame it on the lack of warm-up and practice. After that, it is the result of embarrassment and nervousness because of all the previous doubles and his reputation for the big serve. He registers his feelings out loud each time he double-faults.

The rest of Wilhelm's game is consistent with his serve approach. He runs up after each serve because that is what he always used to do, that is the way he was taught, and that is the way he knows tennis should be played. That is the way pro tennis should be played, but not the way ordinary tennis—the game he is in—should be played. This is illustrated by the fact that when he runs up after that second easy serve he is very often caught halfway, and the return of his modest serve is surprisingly difficult for him to pick up at his feet now (Fig. 1). This is nothing like it used to be

Fig. 1. Wilhelm caught in a halfway measure of his own choosing.

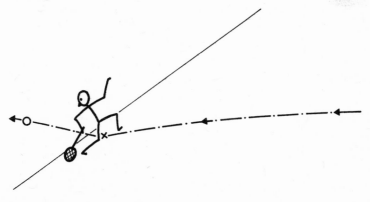

when he was on the team. Or, he runs back for a lob that the receiver sometimes has sent up high while he was running up. He plays the lob by running back, of course, and hits it with great pro snap and ceremony without waiting for a bounce, most often into the net or far long, followed by an "I'm sorry" or a cussword—both annoy his wife.

Wilhelm moves aggressively at the net and often puts away any shot near him. When he does so everyone says, "Good shot," and overlooks his frequently nonsensical poaching. But his partner observes that, equally often, a set-up shot that he should easily put away at the net for the point gets sent into the net or out of the court instead, with a further annoying "Oh, I am sorry," or "Damn it," which long ago caused his partner to invent a standard reply, "n.p.," an efficient abbreviation for the often required "Nobody's perfect."

Alexandra, Wilhelm's wife, plays tennis almost every day with other girls who play about the same kind of game. She is not an athlete type in the sense of having natural timing, great speed, or exceptional power for a girl, but she is steady from playing often ever since she had tennis lessons. She knows what you are supposed to do when you play tennis. That is, she knows what the pro tennis players are supposed to do. She thinks that's what she is supposed to do, not knowing, of course, that she belongs in another category—namely, of tennis players who should do something quite different most of the time.

A straightforward, medium serve to her forehand, she usually returns well, keeping it away from the net player. She never gives any thought to precisely where she wants to return it, as determined by study of the characteristics of the other players. Her backhand is rather inferior compared with her forehand, and a ball to her backhand is much less likely to be returned successfully, especially if she has to work to get into position for it, and if it has a little more steam than average behind it or some spin.

Wilhelm tries to get her to serve to opponent Beethoven's backhand because he notices that Beethoven has considerable difficulty returning the ball on his backhand and at the same time keeping it away from Wilhelm's rather good net-play. But Alexandra cannot choose to serve to the backhand. She just serves, and sometimes it lands backhand and sometimes forehand. If he needles her enough to serve to Beethoven's backhand, she usually gets irritated. Mad enough, that is, so that he will know he should quit directing her play, but not mad enough, she hopes, so that her opponents notice it. They do, but not always, because they are too busy apologizing to each other for their own errors. (They apologize to, rather than direct, each other because they are not married.)

Priscilla's backhand is as good as her forehand, and she is really an athlete type. In fact, she won a swimming contest when she was younger. She plays about once a week. Her serve is easy; she runs up after it, and usually she is caught halfway wishing she were back or forward. Fortunately she is fast, and so she does a kind of running, fore-and-aft, ballet. For some reason completely unrelated to the play, she likes to lob, with no particular part of the opponents' court in mind. If her lob is returned with a lob she expects it to be necessary to keep lobbing—yes, it must always be a lob because somewhere she read that a lob should be responded to with a lob. She does this religiously, wasting most of her advantage of speed and timing and her good backhand strokes.

Beethoven, her partner, is the youngest member of the group and, perhaps, potentially the best player. He plays two or three times a week, and hits every ball hard. Most often he hits the top of the net on his side, although some balls go past the base line and many of those are rather wide. Beethoven is particularly annoyed with balls that come over easy. He complains that they do not bounce high enough. He cannot get a good swing at them, but he hits them hard anyway. These low ones always go into the net (Fig. 2).

Fig. 2. Beethoven hits every ball hard (including soft low ones) right into the net.

Now, as we watch this game of ordinary tennis, we notice that it is a reasonably fast game. The ball goes back and forth, the players are generally excited, moving about and trying very hard, and the ball is hit well a good fraction of the time. We even observe a brilliant return on occasion, and a beautiful placement, sometimes one apparently well-conceived a play ahead.

However, far more often, dominating the play are the errors. A nicely placed hard serve that aces the receiver is rare. But if it happens, it is followed by doubles or by an easy serve that is returned casually, with the server following up by hitting the cinch return ball sloppily wide. Easy balls that should have been put away with ease by the net man are allowed to go by. A sensational run-up is achieved by a player who heroically picks up a ball that just makes it over the net, but who then sends the ball furiously long and out. A net player returns an easy ball, not for a well-angled point, but, unnecessarily, for an easy second chance to the one place in the court where the opponent is ready to handle that second chance. And, as a next action, that second chance is delivered right back to the same net player to give him *his* second. To these errors, we could add the loosely held rackets and, finally, the wood shots,* which in substance and in spirit symbolize this book (see Fig. 3).

How can we distinguish in a basic way between these two tennises that we have nicknamed "pro" tennis and "ordinary" tennis? They are different fundamentally in the guiding concept that ought to be in the minds of the players as they are engaged in trying to win points, which, in common, both games require for victory.

Fig. 3. Jumping interception of opponent's return (that would clearly have been wide by a mile) after a remarkable cross-court poach in front of one's amazed partner, by use of "racket edge" reflection wood shot, producing a sharply angled, perfect net ball that drips off the net to become a "line catcher" for the point. Truly a masterpiece of mediocrity skillfully integrating the highest development of misconceptions with violation of the law of probability.

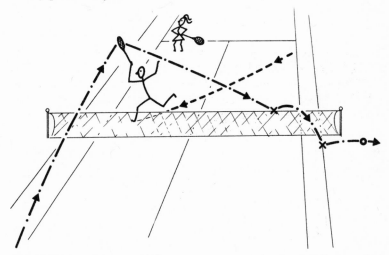

* A tried and true ordinary player can hit the ball on the wood rather than the strings, even with a metal racket. I have done it many times.

In pro tennis the idea is to hit the ball so hard or place it so well, or both, that it either cannot be returned or else, if returned, provides an opportunity to guarantee that the opponent will not be able to return the next shot. With this idea in mind, all other details follow—where to stand, how to hit the ball, where to hit, how to practice the game and make yourself more skillful, how to study your opponent, where to put the emphasis of your time, resources, and skill.

In ordinary tennis you win quite differently. If you want to score points in ordinary tennis, and to enjoy the game more, you ought to have clearly in mind a different guiding principle for the securing of points in that different game. In ordinary tennis, points are made as a result of your opponent's errors. The idea of the game is to make fewer errors than your opponent. From this basic principle follow where and how to hit the ball, where to stand, what strokes to favor, and how to apply your time and energy so as to win more matches.

We must be very clear about this distinction. In pro tennis we must not consider it an error when a player hits the ball into the net if he has been so maneuvered by the skillful strokes of his opponent that he has all he can do to get his racket on the ball. We credit that, instead, to the good offensive playing of his opponent. Our man has, in other words, been forced into an error.

On the other hand, when we speak of the chief characteristic of ordinary tennis as being founded on errors, we mean botches that are unprovoked, unforced, not even encouraged most of the time, by the other side. Ordinary tennis consists in large part of a wide assortment of errors that can be gloriously and exclusively claimed by the person who committed them as all his own. The only contribution made by the opponent is to keep the ball in play, thus offering to the ordinary player an irresistible attraction to the making of errors, most of them unnecessary, many of them stupid, all somewhat embarrassing, and none of them intended to be the way in which victory is to be achieved in tennis, as written in the official description of the game.

This book is written for ordinary players. It is contemplated that, after careful study and application of the principles in this book, some ordinary players who attempt such effort will become "ex-ordinary," others will remain ordinary —all will enjoy the game more. I warn you, however, that the first step is to recognize your limitations. This is difficult for most people (particularly tennis players—after all, it takes a certain amount of confidence just to get out on a tennis court). The situation is not unlike trying to convince a heavy drinker to consider the possibility that he might be an alcoholic.

Perhaps accepting the idea that ordinary tennis is your game would be easier if you reflected for a moment that it is possible to be, let us say, only a bit ordinary. Perhaps you really are a pro player. You have natural speed and timing and form and a deep understanding of the game. You are only off form. You are temporarily making more errors than befits your game. You have become a little erratic. But all that will be fixed. So darned if you are about to give up membership in the pro circuit to enter the circle of the average or ordinary.

My answer to that is, "Fine, but you are still eligible." You have nothing whatever to lose by pretending "temporarily" that what you are capable of from here on out is ordinary tennis, and deciding to become very expert at it. Master the "let them err" approach. Consider: Very few people are going to read and hence learn from this book that there are two games. Most tennis players whom you know will not be so fortunate. They will go on in confusion about their play, and so they will continue to judge you, as they do now, entirely by whether or not you win. You will win your matches more often, and they will not remember the details because ordinary players never do. They will just know that Algernon (if that is your name) always wins, and they will want to be your partner. (Here again, we assume doubles. There is just no sense in singles in the ordinary tennis family, not any more sense than in increasing the dimensions of the court to improve your doubles game. To cover that entire area on one side by yourself requires a combination of speed, timing, and form, which—if you possessed it—would make you ineligible for qualification as an ordinary player. If you play singles, it should be for the purpose of practicing the strokes that you will put to good use in your doubles—and that is not easy because the situation is so entirely different. So if you insist on playing singles, you will lack the available new tools for expertness in ordinary tennis that we are about to discuss and that are, by logic and reason, restricted only to doubles play. You shall have to be content with simply playing a continuation of your miserable game of singles.)

Many times in the past, experts in tennis have studied the work of the most outstanding players of the game and have made notes of the way in which they win their points. Championship matches at Wimbledon and for the Davis Cup have been noted, and statistical results analyzed. Presumedly, these data are offered as a guide for those who wish to play tennis well. Thus, you find that some of the time points are made by well-placed volleys or by service aces, and at other times by passing shots, or by remarkable lobs into the corners, and, of course, by overhead smashes at the net. But these analyses, all intended to be useful to tennis players, assume that the players who will emulate the top players are playing the same game as the pros. This is the game we have named pro tennis, which is characterized by trying to hit the ball in such a way as to make points by the exceptional qualities of the trajectory of the ball. It has limited relationship with ordinary tennis.

We need to do something similar for ordinary tennis, now

that we have made the exciting discovery that such a different game exists and that it is indeed a more commonly, though inadvertently, played game than pro tennis. It may be hard to picture a game as being played by people who think they are playing a different game. But that does not change the facts. The facts are that last year over a million tennis matches took place, played by men, women, and children on public and private courts, indoors and out, night and day, which must be characterized as ordinary tennis. All the participants were aiming for, or thought they were playing, the game we call pro tennis. Each in his own way was trying to base his game on the general concepts he understands as constituting the game of tennis. But they constitute only the game of pro tennis.

These folks are busily engaged in matches that will be won or lost according to a contest of true, unforced, unfettered errors; the brilliant or well-placed shots will be very much in the minority. The side with the fewest silly errors will win the game.

A look at the statistics of the million plus games played last year is convincing. Of all the dumb errors dominating the games played, easy balls hit into the net, throughout the game from first return of service on through match point, led the list. And I mean *easy* balls—that is, balls that might have enjoyed some fairly good speed in their travel, but arrived with such timing, location, height, and velocity that the typical player who sent them into the net could just as easily have hit them up and over the net and kept the ball in play. Service doubles were common in these games, of course, but more points were scored because of the spurious, uncontrolled, and hence erroneous hitting of other readily manageable balls outside of the court, wide and long. High on the list also were failures to hit the ball at all, or hitting it on the wood when there were plenty of strings available on the racket. Waving at the ball rather than hitting it and using

the oncoming ball for the purpose of an accidental adjustment of the grip on the racket rather than for the purpose of
return, also accounted for a good fraction of errors.

The principle is easy. If you want to improve your score
in ordinary tennis, start giving attention to stopping these
errors, particularly the large fraction of imbecilic ones. When
you are well along with that approach, you might ask yourself whether you should give attention to the rules guiding
the other game, pro tennis—that is, whether or not you have
the aptitude, time, opportunity, and patience to learn to play
the different game, which you thought, up until now, you
were playing.

How can you tell if you are an ordinary tennis player, or
are destined to be? Here are a few criteria. There are many
more. To qualify you need not possess all the characteristics
listed below. Any one of them gives you a bid for "ordinary."
Any two provide excellent odds that you belong in that
category. Three constitute an absolute guarantee of complete
mediocrity.

Generally you are ordinary if:

1. You have a punk backhand.
2. When you play net, you do little but stand around and
   never get into the game.
3. When you serve, you rarely get your first "hard" ball in.
4. You regularly serve one or two double faults in every
   game you serve.
5. You play only on occasional weekends—only guys like
   Gonzales can avoid being ordinary if they do not practice.
6. You hit many shots on the wood.
7. You hit many easy ones into the net.
8. You play with mediocre players.
9. You frequently return medium or easy serves to their net
   man.
10. You cannot serve to the receiver's forehand or backhand
    at will.

11. When you take your racket to the tennis store for service, you ask not to have it restrung, but rather that it be re-wooded.
12. You often wish someone would invent a racket with the strings on the outside and the wood on the inside.
13. You often do not realize that your shoelaces are untied.
14. You play in the rain.

2

The Triple Fault

SERVING IS THE only legal way to get the game started. It is also the only chance you ever get as a player to lose the point absolutely and totally all by yourself, without any help from a partner or an opponent. The net is helpful to the server in losing the point, standing, as it does, between him and the limited little area into which he must put the ball. A certain amount of practiced clumsiness also helps. But there are some other things that mediocre players can do to lose the point and do do again and again. These additional techniques are indulged in because the server does not understand the difference between ordinary tennis and pro tennis. It is these particular faults in serving that we wish to analyze in this chapter.

To be on the safe side, our approach in this discussion will assume the worst—namely, that you lack the basic qualifications of a pro server: You do not hit the ball terribly hard. You are inclined toward inaccuracy. Your coordination is far from perfect. But even with these charms, it is still possible to get a serve in most of the time, because you get two tries. Moreover, it is possible to do so in such a way that, since you are playing against equally ordinary players, you can be off to a good start in applying the fundamental concept of "ex-ordinary" tennis, which is to give your opponent a chance to win the point for you with his basic and frequent errors.

There is something worse than a double fault for the mediocre server. It is not any worse in points lost because you can lose the point only once. It is simply less forgivable. Hence, I have called this worst pattern of service the triple fault.

The triple fault stems first from a misunderstanding of the function of the serve for ordinary tennis, and from assuming that you should copy the pro player as though you are playing pro tennis. The result of this emulation and the misconception of the game that is being played is that the server oftentimes falls into a set of three faulty actions, the first phase of which stems from the ambition that the first serve be a powerful, cannonball ace. When that fails miserably, which is very, very often, he then has a "safe" serve, the second phase.

Before we mention the third and last botch that completes the triple-fault format, we should note a couple of common occurrences that may further mislead him and cement him firmly into this terrible habit. For one thing, he occasionally gets a powerful first one in. The congratulations that go with this success are tremendous, and the satisfaction he feels in achieving one ace—or maybe two—in five sets sets him up as hero of the day, even if he leads in mediocrity in general and loses point after point as a result of the way in which he serves. The other misleading event is an analysis that he makes. He thinks that if he rarely doubles he is doing all right. He watches as some of his opponents and partners are driven to tragedy by their doubling, and feels quite superior.

In summary, he is dumb and happy with his unsatisfactory situation.

Now what is it that is so unsatisfactory about this? We commence with the fact that his hard first serve does not go in often enough to be worth a darn. Considering how many errors he and his partner and his opponents make in handling easy shots, and how simple it should be to remedy most of those, a sensational serve scoring an occasional ace comes at too high a price. This disproportionate cost results basically from the fact that the failing hard serve is followed by a safe serve that is too doggone easy. It tends to be so safe and so bad, in fact, that (even if the server had not given notice that the easy one is coming next, the first ace attempt having been missed) the receiver has no trouble exploiting it for the point.

This sissy second serve finds the receiver in an improved forward and ready position; since he, unless he is both mediocre and senile, knows that he no longer has to fear a hard serve, he thus anticipates the cinch shot. Moreover, it robs the server of the value of his netman. A netman cannot do very much against the return of an easy serve. The receiver can keep his return away from the netman with the greatest of ease. Or, what can be even worse—embarrassing, too—is that the receiver can return the ball very near the netman for what might, under reasonable circumstances, have been a ready-made opportunity for a good net play—but not when the ball is hit hard at the net player from a position close to him.

The embarrassment is double. The receiver hates to slam back the easy serve too hard into or right past the netman, taking almost unfair advantage. And the netman, of course, usually feels that any ball that in principle he could have reached, had he been faster, he must take the blame for failing to intercept. The real fault lies with the easy server.

Pro tennis played by professionals contains one boring bit of repetition for watchers. The big serve is almost monotonously impossible to handle, and its response gives the server, who has run up, a chance for an equally monotonous, inevitable put-away. So also does the mediocre game, with the mediocre server engaging in the service pattern described, provide a boring game. The difference is that the real pro game is repetitious only for the people who watch. (The audience waits sometimes an hour or more for a serve to be broken between two good players and for some decent long exchanges to take place.) In the case of the mediocre server operating as pictured, it is the players themselves who are bored with the game.

Our discussion up to this point has covered only two steps of the triple fault. Adding the third step is a top accomplishment for the mediocre server who does everything perfectly wrong. To the wasted first effort of an ace that rarely goes in, followed by the second phase, the safe cinch serve that the other side can put away for a point, our master of mediocrity now adds the third and ultimate blunder. This is the run-up after the easy serve to reach the net (Fig. 4). The

Fig. 4. Mediocre server about to embark on execution of a perfect triple fault, the run-up to net after an easy serve, which follows his wasted effort at a service ace.

loveliest fault of all, it renders the server quite impotent as the ball is readily returned to pass him to the right or left accompanied by his late waving at it. Either that, or his soft serve is punched back right at his feet. Very few players, least of all mediocre ones, can run rapidly forward while holding the racket over their feet to cover the ball expected to arrive there.

The whole matter of what you are to do, being an ordinary but not necessarily a mediocre player, after you have served a ball that lands in will be discussed more fully in the following chapters. For the moment, however, we merely wish to say that if you play against a server who goes through this entire triple-fault routine, consider yourself fortunate. You have something to take advantage of because there is no law that says you have to be both mediocre and generous— and giving up at least one of these traits is essential to becoming ex-ordinary.

Back now to what you ought to do instead of the triple fault, at least in the first two steps (in place of the attempted and unlikely ace, followed by the safe and much-too-easy-to-kill second ball). The first thing is to forget that attempted ace. Although this may be too difficult to accept at first, you must, for your particular style, athletic ability, and time to practice, work out the most satisfactory serve for you. What is that serve to be? How shall we describe it? For one thing, this serve cannot be judged as satisfactory if you always get it in. If you've got a "safe" serve that always goes in, then you should abandon it too. However, start with that safe serve, and hit it a little harder. Try for the corners or the back line of the service court. Your proper serve is not one that is good all of the time. So take your safe, sure shot, and push it a little, even though this will deliver it long or wide or into the net, say, once in three or four times.

Suppose you have worked this out so that your serve does go in, on the average, three times out of four. Remember,

. That means if you fault once in four
fault only once in sixteen points. Most
seven plays. (That allows for a couple
d "ads" before the game is won.) In a
ore, say, "six-two") you will serve twice,
...at whole set, on the average, you will double fault
...ce if you get your ball in three out of four times.

In accepting that one double fault, look at all that you
have to gain. First, because your serve will be good the first
time, three times out of four, your opponent can take no
chances on where he stands, and he is in the same situation
for your second serve, which by our approach is no different
from your first. No longer can he relax while your ace
fails and your sure-to-follow easy serve presents itself to be
exploited. He must reckon with each serve as having a chance
to embarrass him. And, remember, he is also ordinary, and
often hits an ordinary serve badly. For each serve now in
which you have tried harder, as opposed to your previous
safe second serve, there is a little additional placement and
speed and perhaps some spin. He gets a chance to put to
work his own developed ability to make errors, to improve
your score at his expense. The receiver of the serve is standing there, willing and more anxious than he is aware to help
you win. But you do have to meet him partway.

Now, how can you best depart from the triple-fault pattern, to the much more sensible and satisfying "get the first
one in three out of four times" pattern? This, we take up next.

3

The Myth of the Backhand Grip

To SERVE A ball, it might appear that the first step is to hit it. That is nearly right. Unfortunately, there are some things even before that—where to stand when you serve, and what your grip on the racket is to be for serve. Let's take the matter of the grip first. Here, in order to make you a first-class ex-ordinary player, we need to demolish a myth that has been a source of disturbance to ordinary tennis players for many years.

Big game pro-tennis players long ago discovered that for best service they should grasp the racket in the same rotation of the hand and fingers in relationship to the two faces of the racket as they use in their powerful backhand drives. One might superficially have guessed, until the question came up, that the forehand grip was used in the service.

The reason for this is not too difficult to see (although with the aid of the accompanying diagrams, we may succeed in making it quite hard for the reader who hates to look at

34

diagrams, particularly accompanying ones that interfere with a quick reading of the text). Anyway, look at the five ball-and-racket pairs that make up Figure 5. In these five figures, the same racket and the same ball are pictured in successive positions in time from A to E, starting as the ball is first caught by the racket and ending as it is sent forth toward the opponent.

Notice that the racket is not facing the ball head-on, directly, but comes in and "cuts" into it on quite an angle. This is the result of a combination of things, including that backhand grip and, of course, the stroke or swing that is

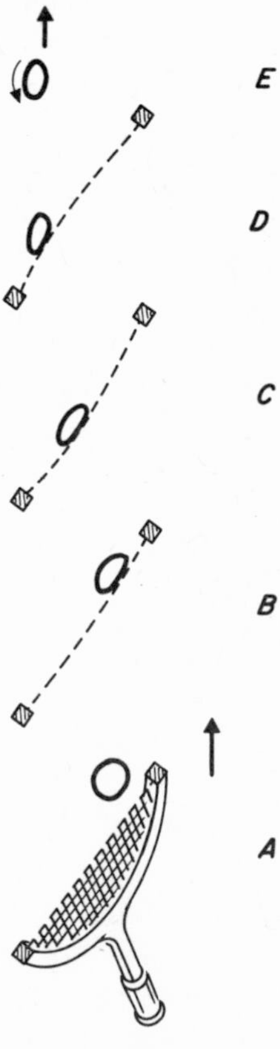

Fig. 5. The racket (shown in cross section) smashes into the ball in a powerful serve.

natural to a server who gets his racket back behind him, his elbow bent way back, and then with a beautiful combination of speed and strength brings that racket into the ball in a way the ball does not soon forget. The shocking experience of the ball is paralleled by a severe traumatic effect on the strings of the racket, so great is the impact of the racket on the ball and vice versa, and the momentum the racket and its motion impart to the ball.

Position A is just before the ball is struck. Position B shows the ball caught and flattened by the initial collision, with the strings yielding at the same time. C, the racket has moved forward and is carrying the ball along in its sweep. Because of the angle of the face of the racket, the great friction of the flattened ball against the strings, and the increasing speed of the racket, the ball is wiped and rolled and further flattened, and slid along the strings even as it is carried forward on the racket. Under the power of this serve you have to think of the ball as being like a resilient putty.

By now the ball is in terrible shape—no longer a sphere, and the strings have been pushed back and stretched (D). At about this point, three things happen almost at once to give the ball a tremendous surge forward in velocity. First, the ball itself, having been compressed into a puzzled egg shape, is ready to react and rebound to try to get back to being a sphere. It would do this if you could just squeeze it down against a concrete floor and let go. Second, the strings of the racket, presumably very tight, have nevertheless been distorted by the impact and, like a powerful spring, are ready to spring back to push out the intruding ball forcibly (D). Third, the ball is carried by the racket, which is now suddenly moving at increasingly high speed, particularly just before the ball is released, as the arm, wrist, elbow, shoulders —the whole body—of this powerful server snap the racket around with the ball near the top of a mad arc of high velocity.

The misshaped ball shoots forward like a missile fired from a gun, spinning, rotating, also changing its shape as it goes, a cannonball with some peculiar curves added (E). When it hits the ground, its odd shape and spin cause the reaction with the ground to be peculiar also. The ball bounces erratically and is very difficult to return. The scenario up to this point constitutes much of the story of pro tennis, so dominant is the effect of this service in beginning each play.

But what has any of this to do with ordinary tennis? The answer is: absolutely nothing, except for one thing, the usual thing—the misunderstanding that associates this pro practice with practice in general, the pervasive notion in the minds of most players that they are supposed to be playing pro tennis. I might say that even if, as an ordinary player, you have the physical capability of executing just this kind of cannonball service—even if basically you have the speed and strength and coordination to pull it off—you still should not be doing it unless you practice often enough to get the timing of the whole operation down. Do not do it unless (as explained in the previous chapter) your success ratio is significant. If, indeed, you can put such an ace in—well, let's say, at least half the time or, at the extreme, a third of the time—then you possess such overall athletic ability and are in such a condition of practice that you do not qualify as an ordinary player. This is not your book—go no farther. If you like to read, try historical novels.

Despite this state of affairs, many teachers continue to press the backhand grip, which feels so awkward to the average player, the run-up after serve, and a few other concepts appropriate to pro tennis on their clearly permanently mediocre students. The implication is that this is the way one plays tennis, and if you want to learn to play tennis you must learn to play this way. Not so. This is the way you play pro tennis, if you happen to have what it takes to play pro tennis. If you have not and you are a deserving member of the ordinary class, then let's see what happens if you use the backhand grip.

Back to the diagrams. Look at Figure 6, which, to get our principles established, shows a tennis ball dropped casually on a concrete floor. It hits the floor in a straight-line drop and bounces straight back up. There is little speed associated with it, and hardly a noticeable distortion of the ball. A microscopic fast-lens photograph would show that the ball bumps into the ground hard enough to cause it to flatten a very tiny amount, and that little bit is enough to give the ball its spring-up. This kind of thing is a "reflection." It does not matter if the ball comes down to hit the floor, or if the floor were to rise up to hit a stationary ball just hanging in air. The net result is that the ball picks up some velocity by this reflection, and moves up and away from the flat floor after the collision.

Now, imagine that a racket replaces the floor and is caused to run into and hit the ball in an easy serve, with the racket flat as in Figure 7. Here, because the serve is easy, it is as though the ball were dropped on the racket. The ball is reflected back away with an unnoticeable departure from the sphere shape for the ball itself, and also with (assuming a well-strung racket) an unnoticeable deflection of the strings of the racket. So, under these circumstances, the forward velocity of the racket is indeed transmitted to the ball by a reflection process. There is no carrying, or wiping, or twist-

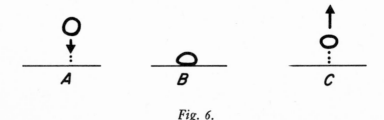

Fig. 6.

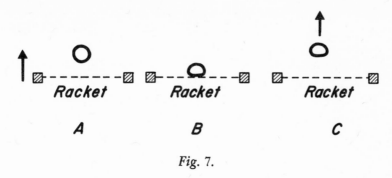

Fig. 7.

ing of the ball. Remember, we are taking an extreme case of an especially easy serve.

To continue with the easy serve, suppose that we turn or angle the racket, and that the racket is still being propelled by the server in the direction of the arrow "R" (for racket), as shown in Figure 8. The ball will leave the racket and head, not in the direction R of the racket, but rather in the direc-

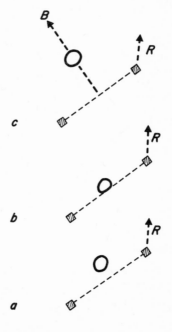

Fig. 8. A ball hit easily by an angled or turned racket moving in the straight-ahead direction "R" (in the sequence of motion from a to b to c) will be reflected off in a new direction—to the left "B."

tion shown by the arrow marked "B" (for ball). A turned racket, in other words, just sends the ball out at an increased angle to the left side, as against the direction of the racket—assuming an easy "reflection" serve. This means that if you turn your racket, and swing with little power in the direction toward your opponent, the ball will go off to your left. Everyone watching may be surprised and impressed by the direction of your serve. The difficulty is that you alone lose the point. Of course, you can correct for this. You can turn and serve in the wrong direction, toward the right, just wrong enough to make the direction of the ball come out correct—i.e., fully compensated. But that is a bit of a handicap for you as a server, somewhat like playing tennis with a periscope.

However, if as an ordinary player you follow the advice of the previous chapter, you will try to develop that "three out of four, first and second are the same" kind of serve. You will hit the ball as hard as you reasonably can, consistent with the idea of meeting that three out of four specification. Then, as you begin to develop some confidence and accuracy, you should also begin to develop a certain amount of angle to your racket. It's good if you can cut into the ball forcefully and distort it, and carry it on your racket for part of the swing, and force your strings to do a little giving and reacting, all of which increase the speed with which the ball will be sent forward and also result in giving your ball some spin.

There is much to be said for a little spin. It definitely disturbs the angle of the bounce, keeps the ball from bouncing so high, makes it more difficult to anticipate where the ball will hit the ground as the receiver watches the server send it forth, and encourages the ordinary, or even mediocre, receiver to hit the ball into the net frequently because he expects a somewhat higher bounce than actually occurs. By the time he wakes up to what is not up and starts lifting the ball up a little bit more, he offers opportunities for your netman to get a good put-away shot. At least, the more your ball spins, the less likely it is that the receiver will kill it for an easy point. The ordinary nonchampion receiver is generally a little bit careless, finds it difficult to concentrate, and is absentmindedly going to follow a ball's trajectory, ignoring the subtleties represented by the spin, of which he becomes aware most of the time only after the bounce.

To get more spin you have to get a little twist, a turning, of your racket. How much your grip should go toward the backhand, however, depends on the strength and speed of your swing into the ball. A mediocre player does not have enough power to make a real, all-the-way, backhand grip pay off. He will just send a weak ball off at an uncontrolled angle to the left.

So far, with regard to getting the ball served, we have encouraged a particular philosophy. This is to get away from the triple-fault pattern that a mediocre player can get into by trying to emulate pro tennis. We have also explained why you should not allow yourself to be sold on going all the way to the backhand grip in an effort to get the ball spinning and off with great power. We are ready now to get the server to stand at the right place, to get the ball thrown up into the air, and to work a little strategy intended to encourage errors by the receiver. For this purpose, we need to consider the travel of the ball away from the server on toward the net, and beyond, to a good bounce point in the receiver's service court. This is what the next chapter will be about.

4

Cannonballs, Micro-Cannonballs, and Bloopers

WE ARE GETTING bolder with our diagrams. This time we open the chapter with a few. Figure 9 shows the profile view of a ball leaving the racket of the server and traveling like a light beam or a bullet, in a straight line, to bounce in the service court. This server is obviously a pro because a ball must be hit pretty hard to have it go like that. With a lot of cut and spin the ball may curve in the path, but it will still be fast.

On an easier, more ordinary serve (Fig. 10), the ball is sent forward on what looks like a fairly straight line for the first part of its travel. Then it loses velocity in going through the air, and is acted on by the force of gravity, which, with a slow ball, has more time to act and be noticeable. Its trajectory—i.e., its curve—starts dropping into a more arclike form, as shown in this drawing. With some spin added, the ball might be directed to just clear the net, then drop for an "in" serve of little bounce, most difficult to kill in return—

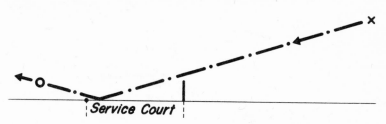

Fig. 9. *The cannonball, superfast, light-beam serve—a nearly straight line—clears the net if it starts high enough.*

Fig. 10. *A medium serve with the usual arcing trajectory clears the net liberally.*

Fig. 11. *The micro-cannonball.*

the "micro-cannonball," an annoying "easy" serve (Fig 11).

Notice that our strong server of Figure 9 has to avoid hitting the net just as much as the rest of us do, and the net places part of the service court in shadow. The part of the server's court that the returned ball can be caused to land in is the back portion, as indicated in Figure 12. Notice, also, that the higher the point off the ground at which the ball leaves the racket, the greater is this available area, this back portion

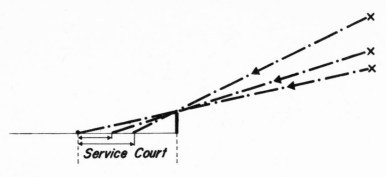

Fig. 12. On a hard, straight-line serve, the higher the point of departure of the ball from the server's racket, the greater the margin of safe area in the receiver's service court.

of the service court that is not hidden by the net. A midget with a bullet serve might be quite frustrated. Even though he jumps and hits the ball at the highest point his racket strings can reach, and succeeds because of his skill and strength in getting a strong straight-line shot, he has only a tiny little bit of margin in which to work, as indicated in Figure 12. His ball starts from too low a height above the ground, and as a result the net shields and withholds from him the whole service court.

The moral of all this geometry is that if you are going to serve with a light-beam type of trajectory, then it is rather important to hit the ball from a high point, the higher the better. Simply, you have a lot more service court to serve into, if you do that.

But the ordinary player does not hit balls like that. The travel lines of his ball look more like those shown in Figure 13, ranging from a small curvature to the beautiful and terrible blooper. (According to the dictionary, a blooper is an embarrassing public utterance.) Notice that there are some advantages to arcing rather than employing a straight-line trajectory. (As though you had a choice.) For one thing, a

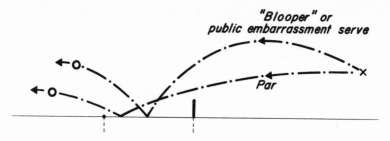

Fig. 13. Mediocre serve profiles.

larger bounce area is available to you. By giving your ball a little lift, you get it over the net and then it arcs down and in. If your serve is easy—not bullet-like, but with a big rising arc that carries it well over the net before it bounces in the service court—then there is no advantage in its originating at the highest possible point over your head. It is almost as though you are sending the ball up to rise and eventually fall on the spot you have selected in the receiver's service box. (Remember pitching horseshoes?) A bullet serve goes for that spot directly, in a straight line; it has to start up high or the net may be in the way. The blooper clears the net so generously that six inches or a foot, more or less, in the height of its starting point does not matter. We hope you do not serve bloopers, and that the trajectory of your effort is closer to that of the cannonball. But if yours has a little bit of blooper or micro-cannonball about it, then the height you want for your throw is what feels good to you for coordination and timing.

Unfortunately, the way you achieve an arcing trajectory is by having a slower ball in the first place. When your slower ball hits, it is going to bounce higher than would a ball with the straight-line trajectory, as illustrated in Figure 14. But an arcing path your ball will surely follow if you are an ordinary server, and you might as well base your game on that assumption. So when everybody keeps telling you

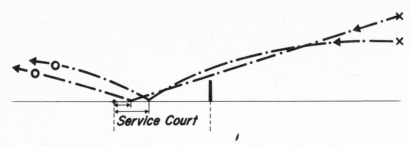

Fig. 14. The arcing trajectory provides a more useful area for an "in" serve, but the ball takes more time in arriving and bounces higher than a hard, straight-line serve.

that you are supposed to throw the ball up as high as possible and hit it at the top point, tell them that you are not Pancho Gonzalez and you are not planning on serving a cannonball, but that your trajectory is arclike and the height really does not matter that much. Then you go about choosing where, over your shoulder and out in front, to hit that ball so that it is natural—nice and handy for your freest serving. Keep hitting it at about that same point each time, so that you get good at it, get a little angle or spin on it, and hit it as hard as you can within the three out of four requirement we have given you.

A surprisingly large fraction of tennis players serve with so much of an arc that even though the serve is not exactly a blooper, it virtually pleads for the receiver to step up and kill it. Watch your mediocre friends serve, and see how often their "par" serve is too long to be good, and yet the ball has cleared the net by several feet. They have thrown away all that margin! Such a server has not even come close to the troublesome net and yet, apparently in an effort to be sure to clear it, he has indulged in a high-arcing, high-bouncing ball that virtually enables the receiver to hit it with an over-head smash (a sure point, if the receiver were not himself mediocre). *Your* opponent may not be so mediocre that he can be relied on always to ruin it rather than to exploit it.

When you see your friends serving in this manner, you just know that they have the wrong idea in their minds of what they are up to. They should really be thinking about hitting the ball directly to and at a point on the ground in the service court, and *not* up so that it will come back and fall on that point. In their minds, the serve path should be as close to a straight line as they can get, the ball propelled forward with good velocity and just missing the net a little. It is sinful to hit the ball with the intention that it will arc over the net and "fall" in. If players are going to have faults, about half of them should be the result of hitting the white band on the top of the net, and the other half should result because the bounce points are outside the service court, either wide or long.

So watch yourself. If you find that you are continually do-ing your faulting with the net sitting there happily and never interrupting your balls, then you are serving up, with too much of an arc. Get that elbow back, and give the racket more of a quick flip; come down harder on that ball. You have some margin to use up, within that three-out-of-four specification we gave you.

A word more is in order concerning the micro-cannonball (Fig. 11). It starts out with good speed on a straight line, then peters out and drops. This action is achieved by a me-dium-hard hit with some spin, but also by consciously direct-ing the ball just above the net. It means a grip that is a com-promise between an ordinary straight hit and the backhand grip's severe cut into the ball. The ball, if it clears the net, falls safely in and bounces only modestly. The micro-cannon-ball will never ace your opponents, but it also cannot be killed because of its low bounce. It is what an ordinary player can do by going just partway toward the cannonball. He cannot go all the way because he lacks the strength, speed, and coordination in his overhand swing. But if he does swing fairly fast and twists and cuts a little, then he has only to concentrate on trying to serve close to the net height, taking his chances on hitting it occasionally. The result will be the effective micro-cannonball.

5

Zip Codes for Special Delivery of Serve

ONCE YOU ARE set with your three-out-of-four medium serve with a limited arc, you will use it for both first and second serve. Your grip is a modest concession toward the pro's backhand grip and no more. Now, where do you stand and to what spot on the ground do you direct your serve? We assume, to begin with, that the extent of your talent toward mediocrity does not make you unable to act on a desire to deliver a serve to either your receiver's forehand or backhand, as you choose. If your accuracy, or rather inaccuracy, and clumsiness are such that it is all you can do just to get the ball somewhere in, within that three-out-of-four specification we are trying to live up to, then you are unforgivably mediocre. You really ought to ponder getting out of the game. Consider long walks, or jogging perhaps, or more time spent listening to good records—but not tennis.

No, we will assume that mediocrity is a temporary condition for you because you simply have not thought about it before. Temporarily, then, before you have developed the ability to control the direction of your modest serve, you ought to stand in a kind of average, in-between position (S in Fig. 15), and more or less direct the ball at the center of the potential bounce area. This is the dotted portion of the service area in Fig. 15. We do not dot the entire service court because the net is in your way and casts a shadow— that is, it shields that portion of the court near it from your serves, unless you're going to send so high a blooper up into the sky that it may come down barely an inch past the net. That is possible, of course, according to the laws of physics, but if you can bring that off, you have the kind of athletic ability that suggests you should not be wasting it in this manner.

While you are still developing the ability to deliver your serve to a receiver's backhand or forehand, as you will it, keep in mind that the average receiver's backhand is weaker than his forehand. Try to serve to his backhand. Don't worry about occasionally fooling him by serving to his forehand. You will, even if you try for his backhand, accidentally get enough serves over to the forehand without carrying such complex strategy codes in your mind.

Now we are ready to suppose that you have earned the title "ex-ordinary" from the low end up. You have worked up, or you will work up, and will be able three out of four times, not only to get the serve in, but to place it to either the backhand or the forehand court of your receiver. Let us take, in turn, each of the possibilities—first, serving from your forehand side of your court to your receiver's forehand or backhand, as we shall specify. Then we shall take up another pair of cases—namely, your serving from your backhand to your receiver's forehand or backhand. Thus, there are four cases in all to handle. (This assumes you are right-handed and so is your opponent. If you are left-handed and he is right-handed, or he is left-handed and you are right-

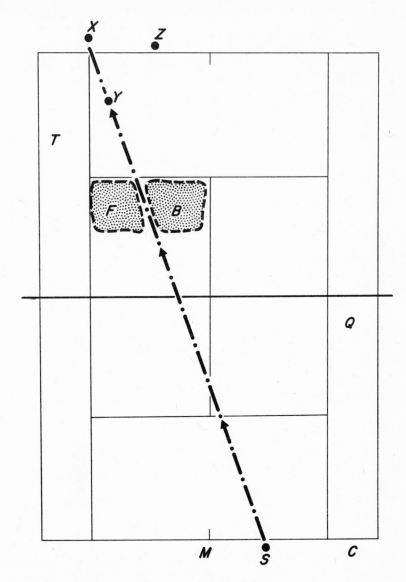

Fig. 15.

handed, then you have to reverse everything we say from now on. Sometimes you need to use a mirror-image. If you cannot make these translations, I have several alternative suggestions: Refuse to play with people who do not line up properly in this respect—don't let southpaws on the court unless you and the others are the same. Or put charts along the wall of the tennis court, like the idiot cards used to feed words to singers on television programs. Or—and it will not hurt my feelings, since you have already bought this book— forget the whole thing.)

Let us start with serving from your forehand, and place you in the median position, S in Figure 15. A little geometry that you do not have to puzzle over (you can take my word for it) roughly divides the area in which the ball is likely to bounce into two equal areas—B for backhand, and F for forehand, as seen by your receiver. If you start from that median position rather than an extreme one, such as the very center of the court, M in the diagram, or way over in the corner at C, your receiver does not know whether you are going to try for his forehand or backhand. He should, therefore, if he is equally well equipped from both sides, locate himself more or less along the dotted line that separates the two areas, the line labeled "Centerline" in the diagram. If your serve is strong, he should get back to about X; if not, he should move up, perhaps, to about Y.

It would seem to be most sensible to plan to serve most of the time into B. There are several reasons for this. First of all, the potential descent to mediocrity of your receiver usually is enhanced when he returns a backhand. It pulls him over toward the center of the court, where he can neither do such a wide-angle shot on you in return, nor be likely to be able to embarrass your netman with an alley shot. In fact, as is mentioned later, your netman has a greater advantage when he is dealing with a ball originating near the center than from the side. Moreover, your arcing, medium-fast, "nowhere-near-a-bullet" serve comes faster to B, because B is closer to the server.

Occasionally, though, and deliberately, to keep him guessing, you will want to serve to his forehand—that is, into area F. This is taking a risk. First of all, his forehand is not nearly so bad as his backhand. Also, your ball comes from a longer distance, it arcs more, it is slower, and it bounces higher. It is therefore easier to kill. The receiver can either angle it completely cross-court, possibly embarrassing you if you are not so good at running up and over to your alley on short notice, or he can dump it straight ahead into the other alley at the expense of your netman. Because your netman has to be on his guard about this possibility, he has to stick close to the alley. That leaves you exposed, with as much empty space to cover on your right and left as you could possibly have, in view of his forehand and your high-bounce, long-trip serve giving him plenty of preparation time to choose one or the other.

With all this, it seems obvious that you should be pretty careful about choosing to serve over to his forehand. In fact, it is somewhat surprising how many teachers often encourage you to serve over into that corner. The argument is that your receiver is forced to run way over to his side to return the serve, putting himself at a great disadvantage because he has left so much of the court open behind him. But all that assumes a pretty strong serve on your part, one that has a good chance of catching him by surprise, so that he just lifts it up and returns an easy ball for you or your netman to kill (you, it is surmised, having run up from your serve). If you have so good a serve that you can really hit the corner or the extreme side line of area F with high speed, and then can run up to take his easy return and send it back where he used to be, before he can turn around, then you are at least a candidate for emerging from the ordinary player class to something approaching the indefinite boundary between ex-ordinary and pro tennis. If your service is average, or fairly easy, then you are begging your opponent to win the point by serving to his forehand. Lots of ideas that are fine if you hit the serves and returns hard and are fast and beautifully coordinated are not very good if you are ordinary, and are still less useful if you are mediocre. No one seems to have worried about us mediocre players before.

There is an exception that makes area F occasionally attractive—I mean, in addition to the fact that you do not want always to serve to B. You want the receiver to be as unprepared for B as he might be if you keep him guessing. This exception applies to some players who receive the serve of an ordinary server by standing in the wrong place. In fact, it is the wrong place for just about every server. These imbecilic receivers can easily be identified. They start out thinking that they ought to place themselves in about the middle of the service area. So they stand back at Z (in the diagram), or even a little bit behind it, since they understand that one should stay somewhat behind that service line. Where they got this notion is not completely clear. One theory is that they think this is the center of the area where the balls might come because it is about halfway along the line and just behind the center of the service court. They fail, in other words, to take account of the angle—of where the ball is coming from. They think only about the area where the ball must bounce, and they wish to be behind that area. They also stay back much too far because they expect the ball to be harder than it is, and because they have seen where pro-tennis players stand.

For such a silly player, it is attractive, frankly, to send the ball either into B or into F. The poor lunkhead has to run forward a bit late and try to pick off a ball that, if it typically bounces in the center of the F area, he has to hit way over in the vicinity of T. When you see a sucker like that, give him a forehand right away to try him out; then mix up forehand and backhand after that. Just be sure you do *not* double. It's a sin to do so with such a receiver.

Before we leave the question of serving from your forehand side, let us consider what happens to your serve if you move to the extreme positions previously pointed out—C and M. If you go over to C, in the corner, then for all practical purposes you have signaled to your opponent that you are going to serve to his forehand. It is now much more difficult for you to serve into his backhand because, even when the ball bounces in the center of area B, it is coming at such an angle that it will cross in front of, and be ready for the forehand of, the receiver. The important thing is that he is now ready. He knows that it is his forehand that has to be ready. You may think, as do nonanalytical players who go way over to the corner like that on the forehand side, that you have attained some great advantage—a very severe angle, for example. When the ball bounces in his service court, you think that will draw him over to the side. But, having started from far away, your service arc is now greater than ever, the ball is slower, there is more time for him to move to wherever it is he has to go, and with your high bounce he gets an excellent shot—a fast, easy shot, almost as if he were at the net—right down the alley. Then, with your netman having to be concerned about that possibility, and hugging the alley, the receiver has the option of suddenly hitting the ball to the other side of your netman, down the center, deep into your backhand. And there you are over in the corner, having to rush back to the center, maybe even a bit into your partner's court that he could not defend for you, trying to recover with your weak backhand against that deep, fast shot. Don't do it.

A little better case can be made for going closer to the center for your serve—to M in the diagram. The reason for doing this is to serve straight ahead, into the backhand area B. This procedure is passable for servers who simply have a hard time serving into that backhand area. It will give a quicker—i.e., shorter—time-of-travel trajectory into the receiver's backhand more often than if you stood farther to your right. On the other hand, it has the disadvantage that it almost signals your intention to your opponent. And if his backhand is not all that mediocre, he can dump the ball over to the extreme side, up front at Q in the diagram, and give you a nice little running problem. It is just as bad if you serve into the forehand area F from position M; then, with his strong forehand, he can be expected to put the ball rapidly cross-court into the Q area just as well. So M is a poor position.

Of course, we know that the receiver may not respect our choice of his B and E areas. He may run around his backhand. He may not need to run. He may walk, or even "stand," around his backhand, which is to say that he notes the long time your easy serve takes in transit, and knows he can adjust to the best position if he has to. But this does not change anything. You still want to choose where to deliver your serve and not have it an accident of uncontrolled timing. If he gets too far out of position, you want to give him a ball to the other side and make him work, even if he is faster than you.

Have you ever been bothered by a server who directs a pretty fast ball right at you, so that you have no time to decide which way to move? You cannot play it with the racket over your tummy, and it is neither a forehand nor a backhand serve. It is tough to return. So why do we not recommend this serve strategy? Primarily, because we don't think the ordinary server can do it—or, rather, when you choose to direct your serve either to the forehand or the backhand, it will go down the center accidentally about as often as if you had tried to put it there. Furthermore, to make it pay, your serve has to have real steam. If it does, and accuracy too, then by all means serve right into the receiver's middle occasionally.

Let's take up the whole other side of all this. You are now serving from your backhand side, hopefully with a score of "fifteen-love." Again, we shall first place you in the median position, S in Figure 16, and encourage you to serve most often into the backhand area of your receiver's service court, B in the diagram. You notice there is a difference. When you

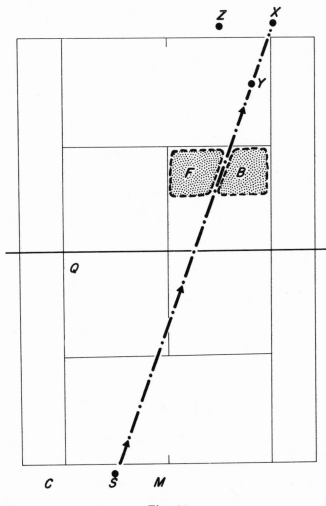

Fig. 16.

serve over to his backhand, he has the big angle opening and he has the possibility of sending the ball directly forward into the alley to embarrass your netman, or making a quick cross-court return into area Q to humiliate you. However, remember that this time you are dealing with your server's backhand, not his forehand. It is a smaller percentage of players who can do these things with their backhand. Your net player can play back just a little, cover more area, if he sees that your serve is bouncing into the receiver's backhand, and still have time to move up and in either direction to cover the alley shot and also protect the middle. Furthermore, a cross-court return to you is going to be a longer time in coming to you, giving you more time to get set. All this depends on the assumption that the receiver's return is slower and softer on his backhand.

For these reasons, we are much more willing to take a generous view of your moving toward your extreme corner, C in Figure 16 for your service position. In this way you protect that corner area; it could otherwise be your backhand Achilles' heel if the ball should be directed there. Moreover, being way over to the left, you can count on being able more often to return the returned serve with your forehand. If you have to do some running up because he sends it just over the net to Q area, almost into the alley, you're closer to where you need to be.

For all the usual reasons, again you should not favor serving more than occasionally into his forehand court, area F in Figure 16. Here, we must assume that he can get his body turned as required and blast that ball down to your corner, presenting you with a backhand problem. Of course, as always, there is something to be said for serving so that the opposition's receiver is brought into the middle portion of the tennis court, area F in this case. It gives your net player more of a chance and cuts down on the extent to which the receiver can angle shots over to your area. So it is not all bad to serve into his forehand when you're serving from your backhand, as we are discussing now. Serving to his backhand is still better, but keep him guessing. Give him a forehand once in four or so times.

Again, we must comment that if your receiver is such a fool as to line himself up on what he, incorrectly, assumes is the center region for defending against your potential serves (back at Z in Fig. 16), then by all means serve to his backhand. Maybe you will finally get him moved over so far, as he keeps arriving too late to pick off your modest serve to the backhand, that you can fool him with a forehand.

6

Socking It to 'Em in Return of Serve

IN PRO TENNIS the powerful advantage of the powerful serve
makes the return of serve critical. Very often the receiver
cannot return the serve at all. Sometimes he just barely gets
his racket on it and, positioned as he is at the base line, is
barely able to return a ball that would win the point only if
the server dropped dead, since it would legally fall within
the court. But the pro server is usually very much alive. In
fact, he is at that moment on his way toward the net, ready
to smash-volley the relatively docile return that the receiver
has been able to muster.

A well-placed return is an essential requirement to break
the serve in pro tennis. Occasionally, a beautifully placed lob
catches the corner behind the server-turned-netman. The lob
has to be both high and fast, and yet stay in. If it is all these
things it will perform the rather remarkable act of scoring
against the pro server. Somewhat more common, although
still unlikely to break the serve on the average, is a fast, low,

passing shot down the side. The basic problem of the receiver is that he has to stand far back and is returning a ball that he has some difficulty getting to most of the time. So he has all he can do to return it at all, let alone to return it well. If, despite these disadvantages, he does get that ball back effectively, then he is on the way to winning the game even though he has started from way back, literally and statistically.

In ordinary tennis it is also true that the return of serve is critical. But beyond this point all comparison ceases. In fact, it is the receiver who has the advantage—that is, he can have the advantage if he gets pro tennis out of his mind and stops positioning himself and reacting in accordance with the precepts of pro tennis.

Let us take this misconception—that pro tennis should be emulated—and picture a typical mediocre player on the courts preparing to receive and return the serve from his equally mediocre opponent. We'll call the receiver Montgomery. Pretending or believing he is playing pro tennis against a pro server, Montgomery positions himself behind the base line and prepares to move rapidly to the right or left in an effort to get his racket on the powerful ace or semiace that he expects. We have already mentioned that such an ace seldom comes from a mediocre player, and in a moment we shall discuss the proper response to make to the mediocre player who occasionally does get his first powerful serve in. First, however, consider the average situation—a first-serve fault and the relatively easier second serve.

So the first serve attempt comes and goes with Montgomery back behind the base line. But, lo and behold, as we watch him we discover that Montgomery moves in not at all, or just a wee bit, in anticipation of the quite different second serve that he should now be preparing himself for. The second serve is generally a ball that bounces well within the service courts, not a bullet-like shot catching the corner or the limits of the service area. It may have a little spin, but not too much to follow if Montgomery keeps his eye on the ball. It will probably have a fairly high arc as it clears the net and a pretty high bounce. If Montgomery has moved up properly in anticipation of all this, and if he watches the server and then the ball very attentively, he can easily position himself to hit the ball well.

But if he remains back and fails to ready himself, he will return with an extreme disadvantage. (See Fig. 17.) No matter how well he hits the ball, if he does it late from behind the base line, then by the time the returned ball reaches the region of the net and beyond, it is not going to be powerful. The server's netman, even if he is only a mediocre one, may be able to move over to intercept it. The server, if the netman has been avoided or is slow, has plenty of time to get himself set for a superior return of the return, particularly if he has not allowed himself to be misled by the ideas of pro tennis.

Fig. 17. Montgomery has again chosen a position too deep for the return of an easy serve.

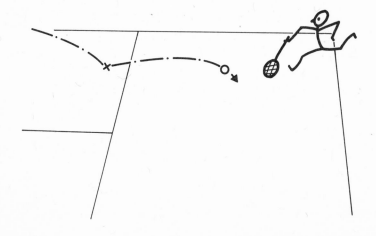

But Montgomery's situation does not end with the simple loss of the point. Since the served ball will bounce far in front of him, and since he has conditioned himself to hold back behind the base line (expecting a much harder serve, or somehow mistakenly believing that is the best place to receive a serve), he will be catching the ball far from its high point on the bounce. He will probably have to lean forward and over clumsily, trying to pick the ball up from the ground (Fig. 17). Montgomery does this often. No wonder he wears out the wood on his racket. Between this kind of return of serve and his typical wood shots, his strings get into the action hardly at all.

It is important to try to hit a ground ball, one of about net height or a little higher, at the crest of its rise after the bounce. As Figure 18 shows, at the peak of its height (B) it is traveling parallel to the ground—that is, on a horizontal path. If you hit it then, with your racket flat and its faces vertical, with a horizontal straight swing, you will send the ball forward horizontally. You can hit it this way, what with everything all lined up, at your hardest pace and direct it with the least difficulty. In fact, at the top of its bounce the ball is making the slowest or least change in its path. It momentarily pauses in its rise as it reverses from going up to going down instead, and seems to wait there for you to sock it firmly.

Contrast this with the situation a moment before (A) or later (C) when the ball is leaving or heading for the ground.

Fig. 18. The ball moves horizontally at the crest of its rise, "B," and is momentarily not changing its height; hence, it is easier to hit well there instead of at "A" or "C."

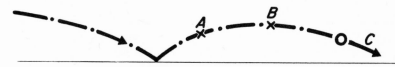

To hit it well, you have to choose a racket opening or tilt that will properly compensate. The amount of adjustment required is not easy for your eye to measure, and what makes the decision far more difficult is the fact that this amount is changing all the time, and rapidly. Even if you get it figured out right, you are now forced to hit the ball up to clear the net, and you must not drive it so hard that it sails over the back boundary line. All in all, then, you have made it tougher to return well, and even when you hit the ball, it will not be so fast a return.

We are, of course, talking about balls that come to you at a height requiring a side swing, not an overhead shot. For a side shot, you can adjust your swing a bit depending on the height of the crest of the bounce, and still use the same concept—namely, hitting the ball hard and flat at the very crest. But if it bounces high, then you have to take it overhead—no choice. If it is low at its crest, bend your knees and still hit it hard from the side only and only slightly up, enough to clear the net. Don't let it get lower so that you are forced to raise up an easy one for them to smash down at you for a point.

While we are discussing how to take a good swing at an ordinary ball with a bounce around net height or a little higher, let us say something for the old folks who remember the 1930 (or thereabouts) heavy top-spin return. These days, with the pros having established such overwhelming reliance on the "big game," the ground stroke game has been neglected. But for those both mediocre and middle-aged with good memories, I say don't be reluctant to indulge in the old 1930 top-spin return. In your side swing, you cause your racket to ride over the ball during the engagement, turning your racket face from vertical to horizontal as you do so. With everything else the same, you can hit a ball with all your might and top spin, clear the net, and be confident it will not go long over the base line. It will fall in, and the darn thing will not bounce (Fig. 19). Don't let anyone shame

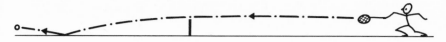

Fig. 19. The 1930 top-spin return—the darn thing doesn't bounce.

you out of this because it's out of style, if you learned it well
in your youth. It is inappropriate for returning the big serve
of a pro, even if you're also a pro, because it uses up time
you don't have in your response. But you're not playing pro
tennis, nor is your server.

We are not going to be as mediocre as Montgomery and
do as he does. We are going to move up forward the right
amount after the first serve, depending upon our experience
with that server, and we are going to hit the ball well. The
next question is, Where to? This is something to keep firmly
in mind as you step up to meet the ball. However, first let us
comment on the less likely, but still interesting, possibility that
the ordinary server opposing you does occasionally put in a
hard first serve. For the extreme case of the grandstand server
who really throws away his first serve by never—or hardly
ever—getting it in, we cannot be criticized much if we simply advise that, as receiver, you be lackadaisical about it.
Make a stab at it if it comes in, and don't worry too much
if you miss. Let him have the occasional point. It gives him a
boost in morale, especially if he has spent all morning at it and
got maybe only two in—that is, you give him a lot of pleasure
per point lost, which is worthwhile in the interest of sportsmanship, good opponent relations, and so on.

But there is something better that you can do if you are the
receiver facing a pretty good, hard first serve, especially if it
just happens to be a day when your opponent gets quite a few
of those first ones in. Above all, remember that he is still a
bit ordinary, not really a pro. This means that though he can
hit that first ball hard and sometimes get it in, he lacks the

ability to position it to outwit you as you choose your position. He has a timing problem as he throws the ball up high and as he swings down on it hard. Nothing synchronizes quite perfectly with him, and that is why he does not get it in more often. In fact, if you watch him carefully you will notice that when he does deliver a good serve it is because at those times everything happens to correspond and match up right— his swing, his stance, how high he has thrown the ball, and his overall timing. And that special synchronism, when it happens to occur, usually means that the ball hits the same part of your service court.

So the moment you are up against such a player, notice his position and his stroke and make a rough guess whether the ball will be to your forehand or your backhand or about in the center. Then try to position yourself so that, considering your specific weaknesses, you have the best possible chance of returning the ball. This is the first guess on your part. Now watch where the ball lands when he gets the hard one in. Assume that if his first serve comes in hard next time, it will probably be in nearly the same place. If he tries to place it elsewhere, if will either be a fault or a much easier ball. Try it that way. It works.

This means more than deciding to gamble on your backhand or your forehand—or if you guess he is going to hit to your backhand, and you have a very poor backhand, trying to favor that side so that you can use your forehand instead. But while we are at it, let's comment on that very point. More specifically, let's describe a mischievous possibility. Suppose you are Tavistock receiving in the backhand court and you notice that though Romney is capable of frequent aces, when he serves he stands near the corner and always serves to your backhand. Now you know your backhand is very poor, and you have good reason to believe he cannot position his hard first serve. So move over to your extreme left to return the ball with your better forehand (Fig. 20). This

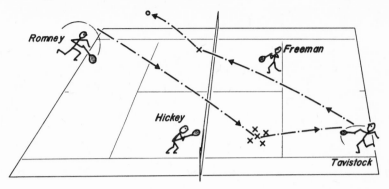

Fig. 20. Tavistock knows that Romney's hard ace serve always comes to the same spot—when it goes in.

is generally enough to throw Romney off completely. You see, he cannot help but notice your rather absurd abandonment of the center and the normal backhand-ready position. If nothing else, your moving over to one extreme side insults Romney's vanity as a "big server." This requires that he respond by trying to send the ball along the center line to your extreme forehand, to catch you too far removed from the scene for getting at the ball. But that will guarantee that he will not get it in. It represents a major change for him to try to place that hard one so unfamiliarly. Besides, he is standing in a rather poor position to achieve a center-line serve. You have taken his one out of five good serves and reduced it, say, to one out of twenty-five—because as he misses, you do it again, and he misses worse the next time. He is sunk for the duration of the entire contest.

Now, back to the subject of where you are going to direct that ball. Remember, our whole postulate is that your opponent's second serve will not be too severe. The server, required to get his second ball to bounce in that little square of yours, is handicapped. With the good arc of his serve, there is a fair chance that it will not hit the limiting lines and will not be too fast. Most often you will have plenty of time to move sideways and even adjust your fore-and-aft position a bit.

So what do you do? The first possibility is to embarrass the netman. On a return of a fair to medium serve, the server's netman is really at a considerable disadvantage. You are returning the ball after having had a chance to position yourself for a good swing. The ball has bounced fairly high in front of you, its height even with the net or higher. You are privileged to catch it at its high point, and the position on the court where you connect with the ball is somewhere between the service line and the base line, so you are up a good distance. Their netman is a little bit like a netman trying to return an opposing netman's good shot. Your windup alone, racket back ready for a powerful drive, should make him nervous. You have a very good chance to hit a hard ball to either side of the server's netman and get away with it.

The advantage is yours when you receive an easy serve, a situation almost opposite to that of the pro-tennis receiver of serve. Let us consider further how to exploit this advantage, taking up, in turn, the two general conditions. One is that you are playing as receiver in the forehand side of the court while your partner covers the backhand half. The other condition is—well—that of your partner when he receives.

On the forehand you should step up to the ball and take a stance as though you were going to hit the ball right down the alley (Fig. 21). Take a good hard look at the alley. Let their netman see you do it. After all, if you are on the forehand side of a medium serve, you can move a little and be really lined up on the alley that is straight ahead. Almost always, you can expect their netman to move over a bit to cover the alley, at least the first time that you do this. Then all you really have to do is swing faster than would be proper for that alley shot, and you will automatically end up with

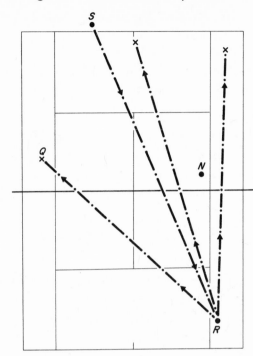

Fig. 21. Glance down the alley, but return more often to the server's back- hand, or cross- court to "Q."

a return to the server. At least you will put the ball on the other side, the center-court side, of the netman, just out of his reach, and present the server with a deep backhand, which he almost always will find difficult to handle (Fig. 21). About the second time you pull this, their netman will not move over to the alley, but rather toward center. This is the time to go right ahead with that planned alley shot. Both these ma- neuvers should often win a point. Of course, being a little bit mediocre, you are going to hit the net some of the time or send the ball beyond the base line because of the overpower represented by your eagerness. However, over a period of time and playing, say, once a week, even a mediocre player can get this kind of shot down very well. After you do, with the server accustomed to guarding the center rear, then and only then should you start mixing in some severe cross-courts to area Q (Fig. 21). You will have dropped mediocrity and be headed for something above ordinary.

While we are still talking about receiving the ball on your forehand side, we should call attention to the opportunity sometimes afforded by the especially easy serve with high arc that is clearly to your forehand, giving you a position even closer to the net. Under these circumstances it is foolish always to return with an ordinary cross-court forehand to the server's forehand, even if you get the ball deep and into the corner. The reason is that the server, even if mediocre and perhaps quite unanalytical, nevertheless is ready for a cross-court. In watching you move well over to your forehand side to drive his serve, and in view of your pattern, he expects your return to be over to his forehand. He is prepared for it mentally, moving over automatically toward his forehand side from his serving position. He will hit the ball back to you at his best speed, right into your backhand, because that's the easiest thing for him to do, what with your having gotten out of position. You will have a problem getting back near the base line as well as getting back toward center to handle a backhand return that is deep.

Instead, you must take advantage of this opportunity, an easy high-arc ball to your forehand, virtually to play net. Hit the ball with your maximum force down the center of their court. After all, it is your forehand side, the ball is pretty high, you're catching it on the crest, and you're up very near the net. So you ought to be able to do a beautiful deep one if you have in mind that this is what you're going to do whenever the opportunity comes. You just keep doing it until you get it down. Their netman, a few feet in front of you, is a sitting duck. He's helpless. Neither he nor the server, who will see the ball pass him on his backhand, will be able to return it, and so you don't have to bother to get back to center. Just wait for the applause.

What is the best thing to do if the server pulls you far, far over to the forehand with an extreme cross-court? In Figure 22, where we depict this, we have shown the server starting from an extreme corner position to emphasize the situation. Remember, we are still talking about a medium or easy serve, not a really hot one. If it is the latter, you are on the defensive. Run like mad and try to get it back any way you can. But if it's an easy serve, then don't be intimidated by the extreme angle, the cross-court path, of the serve. In fact, take advantage of it; you have the initiative. Be happy if you have to hit the ball standing way wide of the court. But—and this is important—do not always return cross-court! That is what everyone does, and so everyone expects it, including the server. The serve is not fast, and he has time to run up and get set to hit your cross-court back to where you were (R in Fig. 22), an extreme backhand for you then, if you *can* get back. Instead, hit a side-swinging drive to the alley corner. The farther off court you are when you do this, the closer to impossible it is for the netman to get between

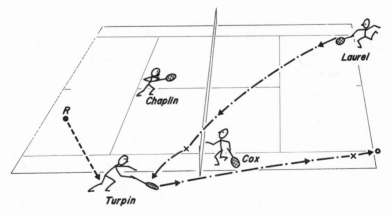

Fig. 22. *Laurel signals an extreme cross-court forehand serve by serving from his corner. The serve is easy. Turpin runs up and surprises the net man, Cox, by an alley drive. Chaplin is pleased.*

you and the spot you aim at—why, he would have to get
off court to stand in your way—he will never do that. (Do
a cross-court later, maybe once, if the server keeps this extreme easy cross-court serve up all day, just to keep them
worried.)

Still on the subject of receiving on the forehand court, let's
consider the return of a ball if it is directed to your backhand.
We realize you could be a player with a good backhand—
that is, one comparable with your forehand. Your backhand
is not exciting or professional, but you are capable of hitting
a strong stroke if you get a chance to get into a good position.
Under these circumstances, you still should not be tempted
to try to hit the ball into the alley, to the right of the netman
as you see him opposing you, because from near the center
of the court it is not at all easy to send the ball into the alley.
It's like a cross-court shot with too narrow a cross-court.
Also, even a mediocre netman stands more or less directly
between you and the alley, as seen in Figure 23. Your backhand has to be pretty powerful to go past him and embarrass
him.

Concentrate, instead, more on the server. Return to him,
doing always one of two things and again keeping him guessing as to which. One of the two is a deep, almost straight-
ahead shot that misses their netman. It will present a backhand return problem for the server.

The other shot is a short little one over the net to your
left into the alley on the server's side, at Q, giving the server
the job of running way up to recover (Fig. 23). Again, we
emphasize that neither of these shots is very good if you take
it from way back. We have to assume that you have moved
up considerably, that the serve is only a medium one, and
that you have gotten yourself into a strong position for a
good speedy return. Otherwise their netman, finding it relatively easy to cover his alley, will watch your slow return,
move toward center as your ball comes forward, stand im-

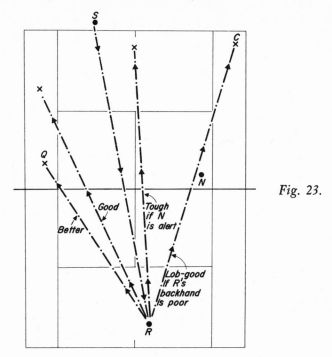

Fig. 23.

mediately in the way of your shot to the server's backhand, and intercept it, angling it away for a sure point.

Your main problem here—that is, when the ball comes to your backhand—is to concentrate on the server and to keep him guessing. You should position yourself primarily for that second shot just described, the one to the alley of the server's forehand at Q and away from their netman. Having set yourself in that way, you then can, after a determined glance over there, choose to swing faster and send the ball straight ahead to the base line and the receiver's backhand, hopefully while he has more or less started to run over to his forehand, having noted your earlier gaze toward Q. It will be, for him, a guessing contest. But it is you who have the initiative and the advantage.

Now let us suppose that your backhand is relatively weak, so that you cannot successfully make either of the two shots described. Your slowness may enable their netman to move in on the straight-ahead shot, or else it may offer plenty of warning and time for the server to move up and recover your shot to his net-alley area at Q. Under these circumstances, there is a better shot for you to use. It is one that is much more effective from this center-court position than from the forehand, and that is why we did not include it before. This is a lob over their netman's head into their deep backhand corner, C in Figure 23.

From your position close to the center of the court, it is difficult for their netman to move back to return your lob even if he is pretty good at going back. Your high lob is not a certain point, but it requires the server to run back behind his netman. Very often, because the server lacks the time, he cannot run around his backhand and must hit back a high bouncing shot from the back of the court off of his backhand. Many players find this especially difficult. They either miss completely, or what they put back is easy to handle. They may even give you one of those cinch net shots that even a mediocre player can move up on and slam away.

For many people with a fairly weak backhand, it is not difficult to lob a medium or easy serve from the backhand side—in fact, some mediocre players find it easier to hit a medium or slow ball up for a good lob from a backhand than from a forehand. They tend to overhit the forehand side. Apparently the very weakness of their backhand ensures that they will not overdo a backhand lob. They simply hit the thing up in a kind of defensive way. But that backhand corner is nasty from the opponent's standpoint. So if you are playing the forehand side of your court and you get a lot of serves to your backhand, it is worth the investment of practicing a lob over their netman's head into their backhand corner. You should master it within a very short time, and you can use it against a pretty strong serve too, one you are forced to take from the base line.

We are ready now to give attention to your partner. Let's change places with him and consider the return of serve if you were he and playing the other backhand court. We assume, as a first example, that though you are not a champion, you have a pretty fair backhand. It may be less powerful and accurate than your forehand, but given a good readiness for receipt of a medium serve, and once over the habit of playing back too far, you are in position to step forward and sideways a little to get a good return back in response to a serve either to your forehand or backhand. Most of the time, as pictured in Figure 24, the ball is served to your backhand when you are handling the backhand court. This, as we have

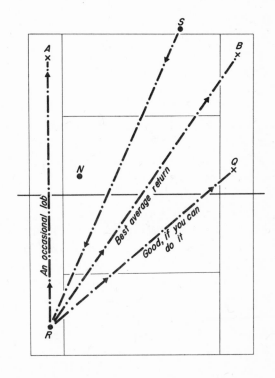

seen earlier, is easier for the server and more likely because
of the way he positions himself. Hence, it is a must on this
side to give high priority to preparation for the return of a
ball to your backhand. What we have said earlier about the
forehand return applies if you can transpose left to right. You
can't? Then let's go through it slowly. If you are over to your
left to return backhand, you should take a quick and early
look ahead at the alley, and position your body so that you
can hit your backhand straight ahead into the alley. And
you should also hit the ball a little early if you so choose,
stepping into it fast to send it cross-court to your opponent's
(the server's) backhand instead.

Of course, if your backhand really is not strong enough,
you should never try this alley shot—unless their net player
in front of you has foolishly started to move while you still
have power of decision and, more specifically, has moved
away from the alley toward the center. Then "sock it to
him." But ordinarily you have to assume that their net player,
with his forehand being his best side, and with your backhand not being very fast, has too good a chance to pick off
your alley attempt and angle an embarrassing little shot over
at your partner's feet. (See Figure 25, where Benz makes
exactly this error.)

From this backhand court, when receiving on your backhand, it is not a good idea to lob over the netman's head
because the server can more easily move over and get a good
return with his forehand. This is not to say that you are
setting up to lose the point. On the other hand, neither are
you exploiting the advantageous receiver's position to try to
make the point. It is far better this time for you to take
advantage of the long cross-court path over to the opposite
corner, your server's backhand (B in Fig. 24). Here you get
set for your best backhand shot over to that corner, concentrating on it every time you get a backhand chance, to build
up your ability to hit the ball clean, strong, long, and deep

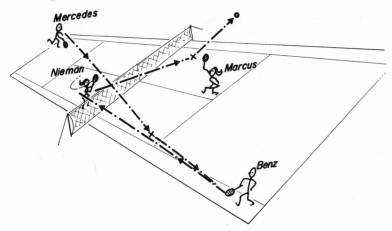

Fig. 25. Mercedes serves to backhand of Benz, who, though he knows his backhand returns are weak, tries an alley shot easily volleyed down hard by Nieman in front of helpless Marcus. If Benz keeps doing this, Marcus will ask him to team with Mercedes so that she can have Nieman as partner.

(Fig. 24). Your server will have a difficult time returning such a shot; he will occasionally miss it completely, and if he gets it he may set up for you or your partner to put it away from near the net.

After you have done this cross-court shot successfully several times, you will tempt their netman to move toward the center to try to intercept it. That is when your good, prepared backhand stance might enable you to pull off something cute. You toss the ball for a lob over to the abandoned back alley (as in A Fig. 24), which previously I have suggested avoiding as too difficult. They're not expecting it now. Just don't do it too often.

Of course, if your backhand gets a little better and surer as a result of concentrating on the long cross-court shot, you can gradually start moving in on the ball earlier in order to achieve almost a net type of angle shot over to the opposite alley (Q) in front of the server. This makes your server run way up. A long run followed by his having to use his backhand will give that server a great deal of trouble. But get the corner long-shot down first before you start pulling it forward. Keep doing it until you are good at it. The investment will pay off.

Still on the subject of the backhand court, what should you do with a ball that comes to your forehand, very near the center line? The first thing we suggest is that you avoid a rather foolish attempt to hit it into the alley to your left. You will botch it. An alley shot from the middle of the court, with their netman more or less stationed between you and the alley as a result of natural geometry, is a difficult thing to accomplish. In fact, it depends almost entirely on their netman's having moved too far into the center, leaving you the whole service court. This you should not bank on. If a ball comes to your forehand, position yourself to drive for the corner to your right and to the server's left or backhand (Fig. 26). Concentrate on that server. Sometimes hit the ball a little early or fast as a surprise, in order to put it straight ahead, right past the netman. Even though it ends up (hopefully) near their base line and dangerously near the good forehand side of the server, he will be expecting it over at his backhand corner where you have always been putting it. He'll be geared to the move in that direction. You probably will confuse him.

Now that we have discussed what you should do in return of service when playing either the forehand or the backhand court, let us go back to emphasize an almost overriding principle: You and the others on the court are ordinary players. This means that the big thing you have to fight is the careless, sloppy, absentminded reaction to a perfectly ordinary serve that you should be able to hit and hit well along the lines just discussed. What you are more likely to do—I'm sure this would be proved by a study of your record over the last few months—is something like the following. You

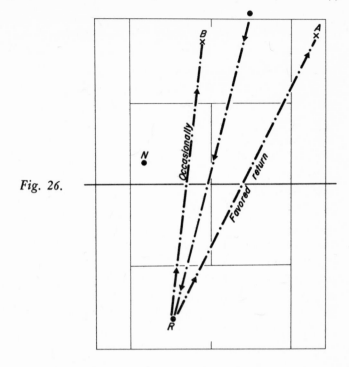

Fig. 26.

will hit back a difficult, hard serve that your often erratic, often mediocre opponent occasionally delivers to you, and be congratulated all around for a marvelous return of what should have been an ace. Then you will turn around and— one out of the next two times—hit a piddling serve into the net or way over the base line for no reason at all. Or you will send up a simple little floater to their netman, who, though no champion, is not charitable either.

The way to fight this tendency is straightforward. You are less likely to do such foolish things, which are really beneath your level of play but which mark mediocrity, if you have in mind what you *want* to do. It is the sudden need for collecting all your senses, based on inadequate preparation, that forces you to face a problem of reaction too complicated for your limited concentration to handle. Thus, you find yourself standing back after that first serve or, in the case of servers who are not strong on any serve, playing back even on the first one, when you ought to be playing up. You fail to keep in the front of your mind the thought that you must conclude quickly whether the serve is to your forehand or backhand. You don't have the recommended responses all set up in your active consciousness for these two possibilities. You are ad-libbing all the way. Sometimes that is fine. But when you get a little tired or your attention is diverted, then your body timing and motions and your observation of your opponents, particularly of their netman, all go berserk, and add up to certain loss of the point.

Keep in mind—this is as important as anything said in this chapter about return of the serve—that your opponent has a very good chance of making a mistake if you will only return that first serve properly. A large fraction of professional games involve three hits at the ball for the point—namely, the serve, a return, and a put-away. For entirely different reasons the typical play of the mediocre teams is also a three-shot point: a serve and a return and a return of the return. As we have said again and again, the scoring is most often the result of an error rather than an exceptionally well-placed or unusually fast ball. After a serve that is generally quite manageable, the returner of serve gets the first chance at an error. If he botches the return at the point, that ends it. If he returns sensibly, which he can do most of the time, then his opponent gets the next chance at an error and will probably come through with one—especially if there has been the right return of that serve to encourage it.

7

Net Nonsense and Non-Stance

A GREAT PHILOSOPHER, who was also incidentally a mediocre tennis player, once put forth the question, "What would chairs look like if your knees bent the other way?" This issue has never been adequately resolved. However, they do not. And so you can sit down, but you can't run backward. If your knees bent the other way, your legs would fold up in your face as you rested on your seat, and you would talk to others while peering around your shoes. There is no way to make a chair for people with backward knee joints. I dare you to invent one. I also dare you to run backward if your knee motion is like that of the rest of us human beings. You can fake it but you can't do it. You can cheat by sidestepping, with your body from the waist up turned forward, your hips and the rest sideways, and your turned head adding a few more degrees. Then, if all the reckonings are in your favor, the optical illusion is that you are making rapid time toward the rear while completely facing the front.

You look as if you are running backward but you are not.

What all this adds up to is that the average player should not plan on covering much area behind him. The pro who can "run backward" is justified in positioning himself more or less in the center of an area, prepared to return balls effectively that may be aimed all around, over, in front of, and behind him. The amateur most consider the region of occupation as largely in front of him (see Fig. 27).

With this general concept in mind, let us consider where to stand at the net, and the important corollary question of where not to be caught standing. Where to stand, in turn, will serve as a starting point for our analysis of properly ordinary net-play. We will start with the situation when your partner is serving. Some of the principles, of course, will apply as well when, legitimately, you move up to the net during the course of the game, a matter to be covered later.

Again, we fall back on the procedure of first eliminating

Fig. 27. Player whose knees bend the other way can run E. while keeping eye on ball coming from N.W. and shoulders turned neatly S.W. so that racket can be held N., back over shoulder, ready for powerful smash put-away shot. You can't do it.

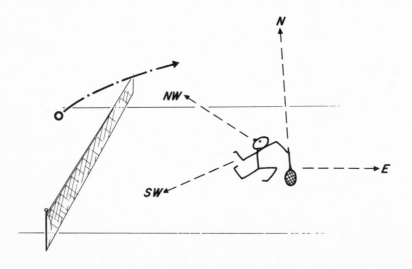

what not to do. The practice to be eliminated, as usual, is that of the pros, whose net-play approach is nonsense for us nonchampion players. The pros, mindful of the fact that it is preferable to cover a substantial area rather than a limited one, and knowing that they have rather unusual speed and agility, choose a net position somewhere near the center of the service court. The deviations in this choice of position depend on the characteristics of the pro's partner's service, and of the stations and anticipated patterns of play of their opponents. But the fundamental thing is that they expect to move from their position, sideways, forward, or backward, with equal skill and speed as seen by the interested but inexpert observer.

Not only is the pro net player equipped with the luxurious options of moving quickly fore and aft and to either side; he can, in addition, play the ball vertically from the ground level up to a good jump height. Described in three dimensions, he is located with his head in the center of a box, which, considering his reach with racket and arm and his jump, stretches from the floor up to about twice his height, covers fifteen feet on each side of him and at least fifteen feet fore and aft (Fig. 28). Within this box, he looks beautiful in whatever he does, and he is a difficult man to pass. A lob over his head, to get by him, has to be a peculiar combination of lob and drive. It must be fast, and must hit the corner or the base line, because otherwise he would leap back for it and catch it before it bounced, for a magnificent slam return, very often a put-away. Similarly, if the ball is reasonably high but in front of him, he will step forward and hit it to a perfect spot for a kill. And if the ball comes low to either side or in front of him, he will direct it over the net, but not much over, maybe an inch or so, so that it presents a low ball to the other side as well, if the placement alone has not fixed the opponent.

But, as we have had occasion to say before, what has all this to do with our play? We cannot move back very fast. The

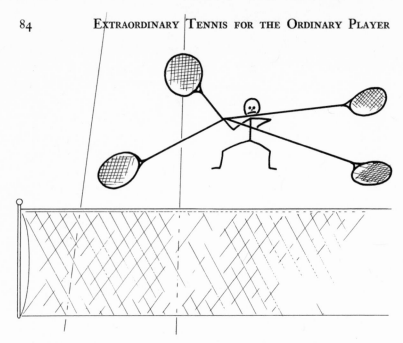

Fig. 28. Pro-type man at the net should not be fooled around with by mediocre receiver of serve.

exception, of course, is an extra-high lob that takes so long to come to earth we can walk back to a good position in the court. And walk or run, it has to be done while looking in the direction from which the ball is coming, not where you are going. This difficulty is just an example. In the case of the mediocre player, all in all, we have to ask exactly what he is doing, playing up there at the net? What can he really hope to accomplish?

A good lob is likely to go over his head, land in before he can get back and get himself rearranged to be able to hit it. What our mediocre player should do, when he is up at the net and the ball goes over his head, is stay put and yell "yours" to his partner (Fig. 29). There is nothing at all wrong with that, you know, because the typical lob is slow, with plenty of warning that it is coming. Your partner, the

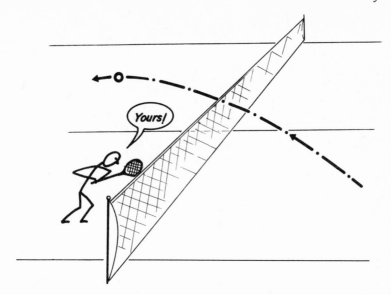

Fig. 29. Mediocre player at net making the correct play in response to a lob over his head.

server, already back at the base line, has only to move over—say twenty feet to left or right—and he has a perfectly good chance at the ball. So, let's get back to the question—why are you up at the net when your partner serves? The answer certainly is not to run back for lobs. Equally, it is not to put yourself into a position where you have an opportunity to wave at balls that come rapidly to either side of you, or to jump or duck if the ball comes at your feet or head.

One reason you are up there is to put away shots that are near you, not too low, and not too hard, the product of your opponent's ordinary play. But to do this you have to hit them properly, and this means positioning yourself properly. What does hitting them properly mean, for you, an average player? It means being able to hit the ball down, at an angle usually, or at your opponent's feet. It specifically does *not* mean being able to volley a low ball that comes near your feet, taking it from the ground and hitting it just an inch or two over the net. That is too tough. Obviously, you cannot hit a ball down hard or reasonably hard over the net unless your racket collides with the ball at some point substantially above the net. The farther away you are from the net, the more difficult it is to hit the ball down. Did I say "more difficult"? In fact, unless your opponent has lifted the ball conveniently high to you in the first place, it may be impossible to hit the ball down and over the net at the same time. Hitting it down is never a problem, presumably, if you're not fussy as to which side of the net the ball comes down on (Fig. 30).

What we are getting at is that you do not want to stand back as far as the pros do when you're playing net. If you do,

Fig. 30. When playing net, hitting a ball downward hard is no problem—unless you want to get it over the net.

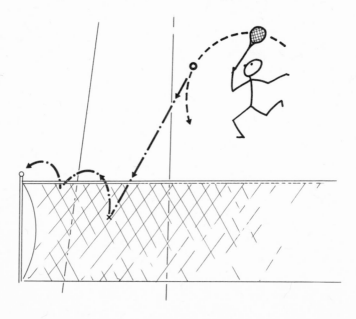

you will be busy trying to return fast low balls before they bounce—and you're not very good at that for it takes exceptional skill to hit them right. What is equally important is that you will not be able to hit other easy "opportunity" balls down for a kill. Stay back too far from the net, and the cinch ball your opponent might raise up to you, which you could easily put away for a point when you are up close to the net, will become a point for him. You will find yourself awkwardly trying to get your racket tilted just right to lift what is now a low ball near the ground or at least below your knees.

An analogy might be helpful here. The professional gunfighter in the Westerns can score a bull's-eye firing from the hip. The mediocre gunfighter needs to hold the gun higher, lining up his eye, the barrel, and the target, if he is to get a reasonable bead on the target (Fig. 31).

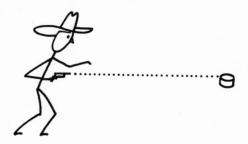

Fig. 31. Pro gunfighter fires accurately from hip. Mediocre gunfighter has to line up the aim on an eye to target line.

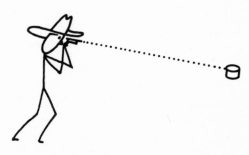

Often, players who recommend that you stand back where a pro does, quite a distance from the net, claim that all you have to do is step forward to meet the ball at the net. You do not have to *be* there, they say, because you can always get there. It sounds good at first. If you stay back you can always go forward and, in addition, they say, when you are back you are set for the high ball that would otherwise go over your head. There is just one little thing they have overlooked: It takes you longer to get to the net spot where the "hit-down" opportunity is, if you stand farther from it (see Fig. 32). Here the option is to play net at N or farther back at P, and in each instance to rush to X to smash the ball down hard at an angle for the point. Line P to X is longer than line N to X, and it gets longer the farther back you stand; no doubt about it. As a mediocre player, you need short runs, not long ones.

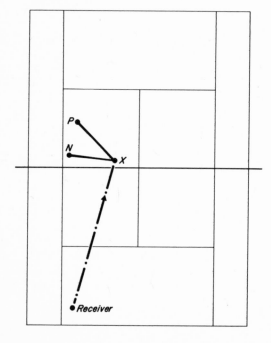

Fig. 32. The distance from P to X is longer than the distance from N to X.

Do not be fooled either by a certain psychological effect that seems to prevail with some mediocre players. These are the ones who are lacking in confidence at the net, and afraid of being close to the receiver of serve on the other side as he goes to swing at the ball. Somehow, they think that if they play back, they have more time to judge where the ball is going and then step into position to intercept it. This is absolutely fallacious. Specifically notice in Figure 32 that the time it takes, from the moment the receiver hits the ball to the moment the ball reaches X, where you need to hit it, is the same, no matter where the net player stands. You can stand on Pike's Peak, or in the wrong court, even behind the server if you wish, but the ball does not care. It takes the same time for the same trip because its travel has nothing to do with where you stand, but rather with the way the ball is hit. Moreover, when you stand here or there or any-where watching the receiver hit the ball, you see exactly the same scene. You have the same opportunity to observe where he is going to hit it and to start moving in that direction whenever, based on that identical observation, you have made your decision to interfere with that ball. So the only differ-ence between whether you stand at N or P in the diagram is the length of the path you have to take, with your particular speed and agility, to get to that same point X, where you are going to hit the ball. Again, because line P-X is longer than line N-X, it will take you longer to get there from P than from N.

Is there, for any other reason, a real advantage to you in playing back farther from the net, trying to emulate the pro who is able in this way to cover a large box of space? Suppose the ball is hit hard and high by the receiver of serve, and let us say—at first, at any rate—almost right to you at the net. If it is continuing upward for a while, as it may very well do if hit pretty hard in a sort of lob drive, then you must react somewhat more quickly if you are near the net than if you are back a bit (and luckily still have it directed right at you). Here is a case where, if indeed you experience the luxury of having the ball come right to you, you have the advantage of the additional time by staying back. On the other hand, this is just about compensated for by several negatives. When you hit the ball from farther back, it is more difficult for you to give it an easy angle. Angle net shots are wonderful, but average players have to be playing up near the net to make them easy to do. Look at Figure 33. The closer you are to the net, the bigger angle you can get automatically. The farther back you are, the smaller the angle before your ball goes out.

Finally, if the ball is hit high but not near you, you still have the old problem of getting to it and being able to hit hard and down at an angle. So you will still, generally speaking, need to move toward the net, whereupon there is that

Fig. 33. Comparison of two positions—one close to the net, the other back—returning the same medium-high ball for a putaway effort.

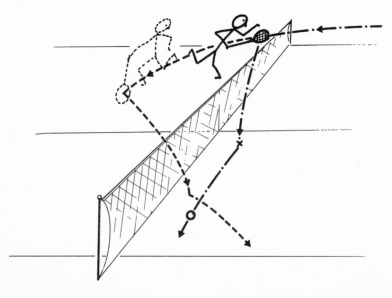

longer diagonal again. It takes you more time to get there.

There are little, but not big, reasons why you should have some slight regret about playing up close to the net. One is that if you are up too close to the net, you will hit the net with your racket some of the time. This will lead to arguments about whether you should be penalized according to the rules, or treated generously, when you do. Who cares about this minor possibility of a minor argument? Another reason is that in the case of a modest lob, a rather poor lob, just a little over your head, you would be better off to be back where you had a chance at it, than to have it go over your head with no chance. That lob, however, usually is going to land so that your partner, the server, can move over for it for a fighting chance most of the time.

We should, of course, cover the situation where the receiver is steady, sneaky, and particularly good at a lob that goes over your head and lands in the corner—particularly if it is the backhand corner on your side—so that your poor partner, the server, has the longest distance to run for it and is put under the worst possible pressure to try to get it back (Fig. 34). What do you do in this case? Well, frankly, standing back five or ten more feet, in a position typical of the pros, is not going to help you. That nasty receiver will still lob it over your head if he can catch the corner. You are not skillful enough to move back fast and give the ball a good strong return from your backhand with your racket way up over your left shoulder. Again then, what do you do? The answer is: Stand all the way back against that kind of receiver. There is nothing so terrible about that. A non-pro player does not always have to play at the net when his partner serves. (See Fig. 34.)

While we are at it, let's admit that sometimes you will get a partner whose service is (at least on that day) particularly bad. He is a triple faulter, or at least a double faulter, in the sense of Chapter 2. His first serve does not go in and his

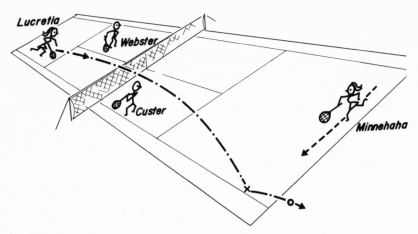

Fig. 34. Lucretia always returns Minnehaha's easy serve with a lob over netman Custer's head to Minnie's backhand corner for the point. Obviously, Custer should abandon the net and take his stand farther back.

second one is too easy. Under these circumstances, although it may be disappointing to have to give up your wonderful net-play, and a little insulting to your partner, it is smart to move on back and get away from the net entirely.

So far in this chapter we have tried to expose some suspected nonsense in your playing at the net when your partner serves, and we have tried to influence your stance on the assumption that your playing is ordinary, at least not exceptionally outstanding, maybe even severely limited. There is one other broad concept, a "non-stance" fundamental of net-play in support of your serving partner, that we must now discuss. This is that you cannot play net at all well if you are committed in your mind to the idea of choosing a position and standing still there. For at least two reasons, you must consider your initial position as a *beginning* one, to be altered the moment you see where your partner is serving the ball and what the receiver on the other side of the net seems to be doing about that serve.

One very direct reason why you should start to move the moment you acquire any data on what is happening is that you want to place yourself in the best position to smash or angle away for a sure point any ball that comes near you. That best position must obviously anticipate how the return of serve is going to be handled by your opponent.

Let's consider some examples, starting with you as Forsythe and your partner Hennessey serving from his forehand side, as indicated in Figure 35. We will assume that Hennessey's serve is medium—not too easy, not too hard. Awaiting the sound of your partner's hitting the ball with his racket to start the point, you (Forsythe) should be looking intently at your opponent Renoir, ready for the serve to be either to his forehand or his backhand. If you see the ball heading for the forehand and Renoir getting set for a forehand return, you almost immediately should start some motion to your left to protect your alley. Remember, we assume that Renoir (though his strongest talent is not tennis) has a pretty good forehand and that the serve is not outstanding. That means that he can, if he chooses, hit the ball at you or to either side of you. Your left is the only side your partner

Fig. 35. Forsythe, eyes fixed on Renoir's eyes, stance, and swing, is preparing to dash to his right but is mindful of the alley.

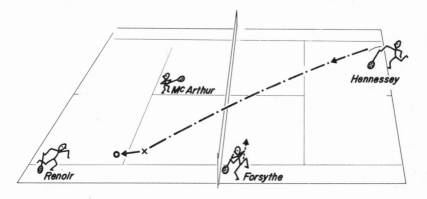

Hennessey cannot be expected to rescue for you. Now, having started to move in that direction with your racket over on your backhand side, ready to block or angle down an alley shot if Renoir tries one, you keep your eyes very much on his eyes and stance and body swing. You may find yourself observing (unless he is a very crafty, fast, and expert deceiver) that Renoir is planning a cross-court shot. As he commences that swing, you will become more certain of it, if that is what he is up to. You should then be moving toward the center of the court, risking the abandonment of your alley. Of course, if you should discover that Renoir, on his forehand return, actually has the ability to make a last-minute switch (as he observes your motion) and to turn his cross-court suddenly into a straight-ahead alley shot, then you must give up any idea of interfering with his cross-court swing and guard your alley. Against such a skilled returner of serve, you are not likely to get by with anticipating him. You must play defensively, and force him to limit himself to the cross-court shot and forget the alley.

But remember, once the man on the other side who is returning the serve has committed himself—body, eyes, and soul—to a cross-court forehand, he is generally unable to extricate himself from that commitment even though he sees that you are moving. This brings us to the second reason why you should regard your initial stance as merely the beginning of a scenario for your activity at the net during that point. Your second, and most often equally valuable, reason for being at the net is to nettle your opponent. We take nettling up in a different light in the next chapter, where we discuss more general net-play. But there is no better way to exploit a position at the net when your partner is serving than to interfere with the smooth and strong swinging of your opponent on his return by forcing him into trying belatedly to change his stance and swing. He will be caused to hit the net or to drive the ball wide. In fact, the nervousness into which you can push him will make his actions clumsier and delayed, and therefore much easier for you to anticipate. Once you get him concerned about trying to put the ball where you are not, it will be much more difficult for him to put it anywhere effectively.

Of course if you have indeed succeeded in moving over toward center as he sends his cross-court forehand, then all you have to do, if you are very near the net as you should be, is give the ball a simple block-angle shove to your right (Fig. 36). This is just a little push at the ball as it tries to go by your right; it is virtually impossible for the other side to return.

What if you observed, while still occupying the same initial position, that your partner Hennessey, still serving from the forehand, is serving along the center line into Renoir's backhand (Fig. 37)? That will give you a special advantage.

Fig. 36. Forsythe, watching Renoir's stance and swing, has correctly judged the return—moved way over and pushed away the ball to his right for a sure point.

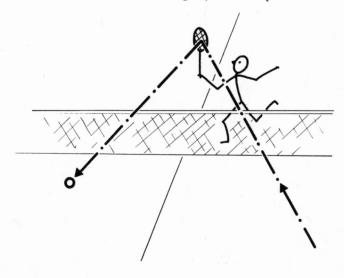

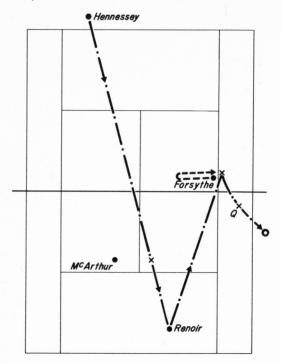

Fig. 37. Weak-back-handed Renoir fool-ishly tries alley shot just because Forsythe is seen to move to-ward the center, which he should.

Renoir does not have a strong backhand; you know that. Also, it is difficult for Renoir to hit an alley shot from near the center of the court, as discussed in an earlier chapter, because you are going to be between him and the alley. You most certainly should be moving toward the center. In fact, as indicated in Figure 37, you (Forsythe) should move over more or less to parallel and be in front of Renoir's position as he goes to hit the ball. You can do that and still be pre-pared to move to your left because his backhand return is unlikely to be a lightning-speed shot. If Renoir tries it, it will probably be a medium- or slow-speed ball, and you can easily move back a bit to your left and push the ball down, angling it to your left to Q (Fig. 37), where there is no third member of the opposition team to do anything about it.

Let us go on to the next play, with your partner Hennessey now serving from your backhand court. Here it is very important for you to get to know the exact skill of your opponent's backhand (McArthur in Fig. 38). Very few average players can take a serve into their backhand and send a strong backhand alley shot down the line in response. If you think McArthur is average, then you don't have to guard your alley quite so much. Thus, Forsythe in Figure 38, feels somewhat freer when he sees McArthur getting the ball to his backhand. Forsythe tries to cover a little bit more area, including being quite ready to move to the center to intercept a cross-court shot. He watches McArthur's stance, position, and swing. Remember, on a backhand return a mediocre player is more likely to be slow, deliberate, late, and clumsy, giving away what he is going to do. If your opponent has this kind of backhand return repertoire, it is utterly absurd for you to stand there like a zombi, as so many mediocre players do, while your opponent, returning from his back-

Fig. 38. McArthur prepares to return a tough backhand; Forsythe prepares to cover a wide area at net. Renoir acts worried.

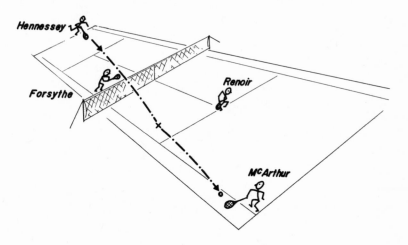

hand, makes it absolutely clear to you where he is directing his return, such as it is. To do so is far from mediocre play on your part. Mediocre means undistinguished and commonplace. To let McArthur send a soft cross-court right by you when you could be putting it away by proper net motion distinguishes you as stupid, not average.

Suppose that your partner serves to McArthur's forehand —toward the center (see Fig. 39). Again assuming only a medium serve rather than a powerful one by your partner Hennessey, you must now take into account that the return of serve may be a good, hard, speedy drive. Furthermore, you have to assume that McArthur has pretty good control and can hit a good forehand, even though some of his concentration is dissipated watching you out of one corner of his eye. Under these circumstances, you (Forsythe) cannot

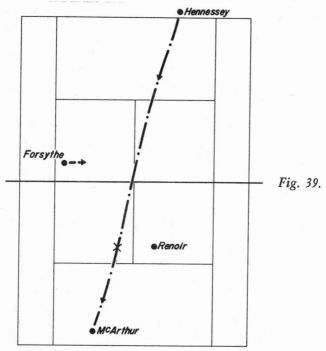

Fig. 39.

completely desert your alley, even though you can be a little more generous in your departure from it than was proper when you were playing the other side. Even with a good forehand, he still does not find it easy to put one over to your alley when you stand between him and it, as indeed you do when he is forced to move toward center (Fig. 39). However, you still want to keep watching McArthur, his eyes and his approach to the ball as well as his body swing. There is no point in your letting him have any more of the court to work with than necessary.

Very frequently, an average-type net player congratulates himself because he has never allowed his opponent to get by with an alley shot, either on the forehand or the backhand side. This net player hugs the alley. If his equally nonchampion opponent tries to put one down the alley, he clobbers it for a point by angling it down and away to the side. But this is really not something to brag about. Specifically, if you are this kind of net player and no alley shot ever gets by you, it means that you are overdoing it. Your opponent is rarely going to try an alley shot on you. He knows that you are going to abandon the rest of the court and stay fixed to protect that alley. You have given him the maximum of time to get set for a good return and a maximum amount of court to do it in. You have given him everything but the narrow alley. And you have provided your partner essentially no support, and have failed to nettle your opponent. All in all, you have probably lost ten times as many points for your side by your neglect as the few you gained by handling that occasional alley shot.

In summary, if you don't give up a few shots down your alley as a result of having moved in anticipation of some other shot, then you are not playing as good a net game as you should be capable of. Of course, maybe your opponent is so slow, or you are so fast at the net and so superior to your opponent, who nevertheless insists on trying to fool you, that you return his shots whether they are to the alley or to the center. You have plenty of time to move to the proper position after he hits the ball. Then so much the better. But it is not Christmas every afternoon on the courts. We are not talking about your looking good at the net because your opponent insists upon making it easy for you.

8

Net Nettling

WE HAVE ALREADY indicated that there are two important reasons for your being at the net, assuming you have not arrived there in confusion and by accident instead of through deliberate intent. The first and obvious one is to drive away the balls that come near you, for the point. You must move with the action to try to make this possible. The other and equally important objective for you as netman is to nettle your opponent, who is concerned with returning a ball to your side. Your position, stance, and motion, and your close attention to your opponent's every action should be calculated not only to limit and control his freedom to return, but also to confuse his strategy and generally influence his playing for the worse.

In the preceding chapter we covered some of these points, but always with the assumption of your playing net while your partner was serving. Now we need to discuss net-play during the playing out of the point. We particularly want to examine the highly useful but seldom discussed role of the player who can rise above the dull fraternity by taking to the net, not for the anticipated smash of an easy ball, but rather more to drive his opponent into a sudden feeling of constraint and hopelessness, which will lead to frenzy and error.

As indicated earlier, for a mediocre player to run up to the net can sometimes be dangerous. We discussed this in particular in connection with the server's doing so after an easy serve. There are, of course, equivalents to that situation during the course of the game. If you or your partner hits an easy ball to one of your opponents—say, right to his fore-hand and just where he happens to be standing in a perfect position, with lots of time to clobber the ball well in return —and if it doesn't even bounce far back in his court, then that is the wrong time for you to run up. But there are other bad times.

One is after you or your partner has hit an easy high floater right to their netman, who is about to hit it down hard at your feet or over to the side. Unless you are possessed of special insight into just where that netman's ball will strike, and how it will bounce after he slams it, which would be at least a minor miracle, then you had better stay back where you are and not run up. You will still lose the point, for it is probably irretrievable, but such chance as remains will be enhanced, you will look less silly, and you will save energy.

The converse of these situations is what we must look for when we move up to the net, if we are of average athletic ability. If you or your partner hits an exceptionally strong, deep ball to your opponent's weak side—usually that means his backhand—and if you see that he must struggle just to get to it, that is the time to move up. For one thing, you have time to go to the net because if the ball is going to be re-turned to you at all, it will be returned without great force and speed. It's going to be a sort of slow sailer, hopefully directly to you or to your partner (heck, you can both run up in this kind of situation). Also, you have time and can take time to consider the situation. It might be that your opponent, though suffering on his way to the ball and very likely to offer a poor return, may, in defense, hit a very high, deep lob. You should do your regretting and anxious awaiting before he does that rather than after.

Consider the diagram of Figure 40, which initially shows Roland back, and indicates that he has directed a very strong and deep ball into the corner of his opponent O'Malley, which O'Malley will take with a backhand. Roland, tentatively expecting O'Malley to offer a modest return, moves

Fig. 40. Roland runs up to put away O'Malley's anticipated weak backhand return to the net, but it turns out to be a strong cross-court shot instead.

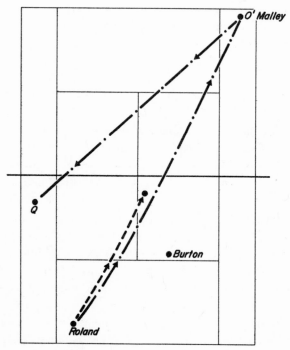

up partway, prepared to go up the rest of the way, even poaching a lot toward center and his partner Burton if the return is seen to be weak enough so that Roland can smash it at the net. If O'Malley surprises him and hits a fast cross-court low ball right back to pass Roland on his backhand side, as shown (Q in Fig. 40), it will teach Roland not to move up the next time against O'Malley. There are lots of mediocre players. Roland should save this maneuver for one of those, one not quite so good as O'Malley. But Roland was dead right in his maneuver if O'Malley is a weak backhand returnee.

A mediocre net player can be much more valuable to his team if there is a mediocre player on the other side who is afraid of net players. The moment you spot this characteristic in one of your opponents—a dread of the netman on the other side—then your net game must change fundamentally. You now clearly have in full play the two purposes of being at the net, which were previously mentioned—to put the ball away for a point if it comes your way, and to position yourself in a way that will nettle and completely destroy the game of your nervous opponent. Under these circumstances, you may position yourself in violation of what might appear to most pro players and many mediocre players (and even to your partner) as sensible net-play positioning.

For example, you may find that your opponent, the fearful type, also has a less than pro-type backhand. Therefore, whenever a ball goes to that opponent's backhand, run up. Do it from wherever you are, and try to place yourself between that player and your entire court. This does not mean that you necessarily position yourself in the middle, but rather between the middle of your court and wherever that player is. The diagram (Fig. 41) shows a number of examples. In the first instance, your opponent is returning from his deep backhand corner P, and if he executes a return despite his nervousness, it may land anywhere in your court.

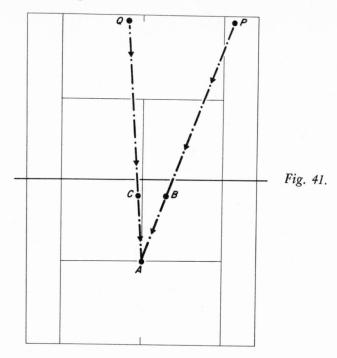

Fig. 41.

The average, or center, is A in the diagram. So position yourself between your opponent and A—namely, at B—even if that means some terrible poaching on your partner. (The exception to this is—well, don't do it when your partner is already at B. We don't need two of you returning the same ball. It is particularly the wrong thing to do to rush to point B when your partner is already there if he is a person who also has mental problems, such as "partner phobia proximus," fear of one's partner being on top of one.) In the other example in Figure 41, we show your weak backhanded and frightened opponent returning from position Q. Here, you want to be in position C, protecting the center of the court.

Remember, the major part of the idea is that the return ball will be slow enough so that you can literally move across

half the court and still get there in time to put the ball away
for the point.

Taking advantage of fear on the part of your opponent
should take you to the net not only when his fragility of
nerves is combined with his having a weak backhand. You
should consider going to the net against such an opponent
even if he has a strong forehand. What you do then is force
him to return the ball always to your partner—he is com-
pelled by his fear to avoid you and anything within fifteen
feet of you. Knowing this, you might as well be carrying a
gigantic shield about thirty feet wide. You can abandon your
alley, or almost do so, because he is so deathly afraid of getting the ball near you he will not try for the alley. You
really have to leave that alley wide, wide open to entice him
to try it. You can force him more and more over to your
partner's side until he errs by hitting wide on that side. The
diagram of Figure 42 shows this. The shaded area is the
area Agatha will avoid. It's what she feels is covered by
Christie's reach. So to her no alley is left, even though
Christie is quite far from his alley. Agatha's mind keeps

*Fig. 42. Agatha, in dread of netman Christie, who has just run
up, hits the ball way wide to the other side.*

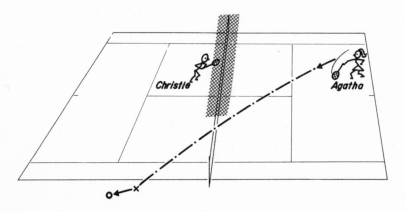

focusing on that remainder of Christie's court that she conceives of as representing Christie's partner, who is playing back. This means that the partner has plenty of warning and can get himself set for return shots. Also, it means that Christie can take some risks of moving over to center early, just as the ball is hit.

This kind of thing can nettle your worried opponent to the extent that soon even her forehand will not be good. And if your partner runs up too—as the opponent goes to hit the ball, that is—so that the opponent sees two netmen, then she will be more than nettled. She will come apart. It is mean to do it.

Of course, your neurotic opponent might be driven defensively to attempt to lob everything, and under those circumstances you should consider moving back from the net slightly in order to discourage a lob. You see, your mediocre opponent has not thought out this business of your being unable to run back much, and she has no appreciation of the fact that you are less effective as you push back from the net. Remember, she is not going to try to return to you anyway; therefore, much of the discussion in Chapter 7 about staying close to the net will not apply when you are playing against the "netophobic" opponent.

9

Lob Liberties

IN PRO TENNIS, a lob has to be a pretty darn good lob to
rescue the player who resorts to it. First of all, he naturally
is not going to hit a lob if his opponent is back. A pro receiver, given a high shot and hence time to get himself into
position, his racket back, his timing perfectly adjusted, can
be expected to send the ball away before the bounce with
such vigor that no return is conceivable. After all, it is like
his ace serve, except that he has the whole court to put it in
rather than a little 20 percent of it, partly shielded by the net,
as happens when he serves. Furthermore, now he is not standing behind the service line but in front of it. You do not lob
to a pro who is back.

The lob is most often something of a defensive rescue shot
in pro tennis. It is what a pro might do when in a weak position, when he can't get a really strong low shot in because one
or both of his opponents are standing almost on top of him
near the net, ready to pounce on it. He hopes that by putting

the ball over the head of the netman or netmen he can get it just barely to land in. If clever, deceitful, and skillful enough, a pro can turn the lob into an offensive point-winning stroke. That's tough, however, because a pro up near the net usually sees what is happening, and since a lob has a relatively long trajectory time (taking time to go up and time to come down), the athletic receiver can generally run back in less time than it takes for the ball to go through its full journey. Usually the lob tried in pro tennis is just a little long when it fails, or catches the opposition by surprise when it succeeds.

There are other interesting pro lob situations, but enough of pro lobs. We bring up these fragments from pro tennis for a reason, but not because they have direct applicability to everyday tennis. It is rather the opposite. Our interest in them stems from the fact that we are all indoctrinated with the guidance that comes from the really good players who are capable of playing championship tennis. We go about our work in our sphere of ordinary tennis handicapped by the conceptions that apply to the pro world but not to ours. Thus, if we are going to discuss lobs in our tennis fraternity, we want first to try to call conspicuous attention to the impression of lobs we may have gained as a result of the powerful influence of the pros, and then quickly contrast this, for added emphasis, with what a lob should be in nonpro tennis.

To mediocre tennis players, lobs offer many attractive opportunities for errors, usually the result of fundamental misconceptions. The idea is to fix it instead so that your opponents make the errors. Some of these errors have to do with what I call the "alternation-lob-syndrome." At least, the particular kind of error associated with this (sometimes) cult and (sometimes) malady comes up often, and we may as well get at it first.

Suppose that, somehow or other, a lob gets started in a mediocre tennis match. You are somewhere in your back court when a high ball originates somewhere in their back court. It is going up high over the net on its way to you. Now if you and your partner are both up at the net at the time, then you ought to keep in mind your basic limitations, call "out" very loudly, and then turn and see where it really lands. If it is out, all is well. If it lands in, then sportsmanship requires that you revise your early call and congratulate your opponent. "Beautiful shot—I was sure it would be out" is good. If you are back and your partner is up, of course it is for you to return the ball. Let's take this unfortunate situation and see it through.

We start with the observation that for the vast majority of lobs served to you while you are in the back court, you have ample time to get yourself in position to return them. Most of the time, that is, even if you wear a crutch, a high lob by a mediocre player takes so long to go up and come down and bounce and then rise again, ready for you to return it, that you can get yourself set for it if you are not up at net. If you prefer forehand or, let us say, if your backhand is thoroughly unreliable, you'll even have time to move another two or three feet—that's all it takes to shift for an overhead stroke from backhand to forehand to return a lob, the width of your shoulders—and hit the ball back forehand. Yes, that's what we said: To hit a high ball forehand rather than backhand obviously requires only that you move over about the width of your shoulders, and that is a tiny fraction of the court width. (A man with tremendously broad shoulders who is also so slow it takes him significant time to move through that equivalent shoulder width of court, who also has to run around his backhand in order to return a lob with his forehand, really ought to stay off the tennis court. It is just too embarrassing. He should go in for wrestling or, perhaps, politics.)

So, almost incidentally here, we have turned up the first rule for handling lobs when you are already in the back court, and that is the only time you will handle them. Mainly, the rule is that as long as you're going to move about to get yourself in position to return the lob, you must not get caught with the need for a backhand return unless you have a good high backhand, which few nonchampion players have.

What do you do about the situation where the lob is not so high—perhaps could have been hit by a decent netman (which you do not happen to have at the moment) if he had just jumped a little bit—and gets over to your backhand back corner rather soon, while you (Harding in Fig. 43) meanwhile have had to start for it from all the way over in the forehand corner? Under such circumstances, I don't consider it basically an error if you do not get there at all, or if, when you do make it and try your miserable backhand, you either fail to return the lob or else deliver it weakly to their netman. They are entitled to the point; congratulate them. It will be one of their few earned points of the match. Why begrudge it to them? Get the rest of your errors down, and do not worry about handling that very difficult shot.

Let's get back to the situation where you are in position to take the lob after the ball has bounced. Again, we must point out what by now should be obvious: A mediocre player

Fig. 43. *Cunningham sends a lob-drive over Stanley's head. No one can blame Harding if she can't get there. Templeton knows the point is won.*

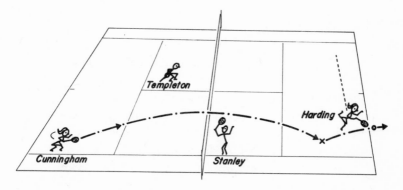

should never take a lob without waiting for the bounce. First, let's make clear that we do not consider a high ball that you can hit by reaching up for it when in position at the net a true lob. Naturally, if one like that comes your way, you slam it now, not after, the bounce. We are speaking, rather, of the high-trajectory lob that goes over the net area and bounces somewhere in the rear of the court, or would do so if you let it.

There are a lot of reasons why you must let the ball bounce. First of all, it might bounce out—and you'd have the point. Second, hitting such a ball as it comes down from on high without waiting for a bounce is a very difficult timing problem. At the end of a year, if your score is better than one in ten you belong in the pro circuit. You will most often hit the ball to the ground on your side, into the net, out, or do a bad wood shot or something, and lose the point.

We will grant that if you are up quite far toward the net, by hitting the ball from that point, instead of waiting for it to bounce and taking it farther back, you may be able to make a nice put-away shot. If you are not near the net, however, the chances are that you will still be able to hit it well after the bounce. After all, you ought to be able to do it because it is very much like serving, except that you have the whole court to put it into. It will not be a powerful smash, for the same reasons that you do not possess a powerful serve. But they are not pros on the other side. You can place it to help them miss it.

This brings us to the question of where to direct your return of a lob that you have positioned yourself for with your forehand. You can choose to drive it or lob it back. By driving it we mean, of course, that you try to hit a lower shot, one just over the net with some pretty good speed on it. We *don't* mean that you will hit it sideways. It is much too hard to try to hit a high bouncing ball with a side stroke because, again, the timing problem is horrible. If you can do it,

you ought to quit reading this book right now and learn a
foreign language or take up advanced calculus in the time
made available; your tennis is already all right.

So if you drive a high bouncing ball rather than lob it,
it will be by a forehand overhead, like your serve, but with
the entire enemy court to choose from for a target. The
first piece of advice here is to give up the idea that you absolutely have to lob it back. Don't get me wrong. There is
nothing wrong with lobbing a lob if, as in Figure 44, one of
your opponents (Symington) is up at the net and the other
one (Dill) is back, particularly if the one who is in the back
(Dill) is over on his forehand side. Then a lob into his backhand corner is your best bet (as Loughborough plays it in
Figure 44). As we said before, Dill *can* run over to get it. He
has plenty of time, and can even hit it out of his forehand
side most often, if he chooses, by running two more feet.

*Fig. 44. Loughborough returns from Dill by sending a lob over
Symington's head to Dill's backhand corner. Ketchum should be
ready to cover the entire net, anticipating a weak return by
Dill; Loughborough should prepare to handle a return lob anywhere.*

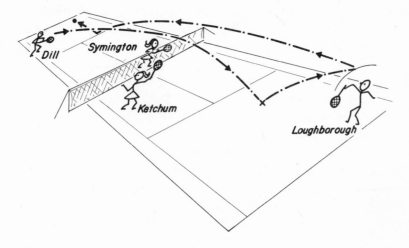

But remember, Dill is not a champion player. He will probably do something fancy or screwy instead of doing the right thing. So just give him a chance to keep returning it. It is your errors we are worrying about right now, not his.

Next, still assuming that you are going to lob it back because there is a strong net player, we must point out there is nothing that compels you (as so many unintelligent lobbers assume to be the case) to keep shifting your return—alternating first to the backhand and then to the forehand corners of the opponents. This "alternation-lob syndrome" has the superficial advantage of giving them a reason to run about on the other side. Unfortunately, it also helps to confuse you because you have to keep getting reset to hit the ball to a different place each time, and you might hit it out. You do have the option, you know, of just hitting it back a second time to the same backhand corner. Especially is this sound if the other side has become accustomed to the idea of oscillating back and forth. They will start going the other way, both their netman and their back-court man, as soon as you start to hit the ball, and they will be caught and have to reverse their field, which is just as annoying to them as it is helpful to you. So be repetitive occasionally and thus minimize the frequency of your errors. (See Figure 45, where Funk and Wagnalls indulge in a silly illustration of the meaning of this practice.)

But don't lob all the time. Consider that you have been practicing serving all your tennis life. When you have yourself in position to handle a ball that is bouncing up high enough so that you can hit it with a good overhand serve stroke, you ought to be able to put a good fast ball into their open areas. This is particularly to be favored if it turns out that at the moment you are pressed for a decision, their net player is over to one side, the other side from you. In fact, if you have received the lob more or less in your corner, you can hit straight down the alley. If that alley happens to

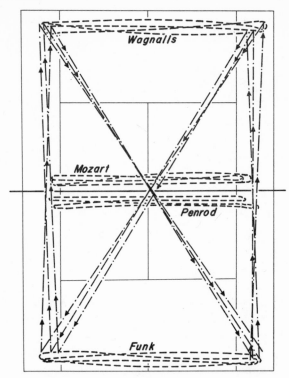

*Fig. 45. Funk and Wagnalls define the "alterna-
tion-lob syndrome."*

be their backhand alley, and if the mediocre opponent in
that area is expecting you to return a lob with a lob, then
this can help him greatly to make an error or miss the ball
entirely (Fig. 46).

What is the worst thing to do with a lob? Returning a lob
by giving a gentle medium-high ball right to the netman is
among the silliest returns. Know yourself if you want to
avoid this. For instance, here is how it can happen to you.
Let's say your regular serve is unfortunately rather easy.
Then your drive return of a lob is likely to be similarly easy.
Any netman, even a mediocre one, can move from one side

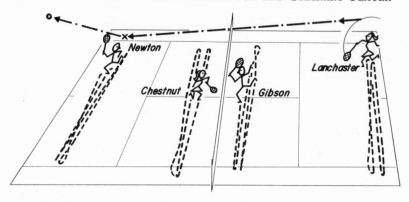

Fig. 46. After several alternating lob exchanges between Lanchaster and Newton, during which Chestnut and Gibson have lost synchronization through fatigue, Lanchaster (mediocre but not dumb) surprises with an alley drive. Newton is annoyed. Chestnut and Gibson are too busy shifting positions to notice.

to the center (and almost to the other side) while this easy ball of yours is in transit. He will get there and put it away. If this is your serve characteristic, then you have no choice but to lob back. Perhaps the idea of returning a lob with a lob was discovered by someone with a terribly slow serve who was continually giving set-up opportunities to the opposition's netman when he returned a lob—until he lobbed back and made a great discovery.

Now consider the situation in which you are returning the lob and both of your opponents are back. There is no possibility of your making them run from one side to the other. They are both positioned to handle your return of their lobs. Here two returns will minimize your playing into their hands with a stupid error. One is to return their lob with a lob of your own, but carefully into the center. Let them fight over it. And if you keep this in mind as something you can easily and frequently do when both their players are back, you will get very accurate at sending forth a good lob that bounces near the base line close to the center of the court. It is a lot easier for you to get good at that than it is to chase back and forth, and make them chase back and forth, to see who will make the first error. They are much more likely to make the error than you if you put your returns into the center, and repeatedly force them to work out which one will handle each return.

Moreover, if neither of them is up near the net, you no longer have to worry about their netman. Under these circumstances, you really ought to put the ball down the center with the closest attainment you can muster to a powerful drive, even if you are an easy server and thus an easy driver from an overhead position. Your drive will be a little steamier, perhaps, than your serve because you don't have to feel so constricted about where you put it. It will bounce farther back near the base line, and they will have trouble figuring out who should try to return it. You can be confident about this one. After all, you do serve, and serving is ordinarily done under conditions of considerable restraint and hardship compared with what you now have open to you as the satisfactory area for your "serve-drive" to bounce in.

Let's shift to a different situation. Suppose that you or your partner has hit a lob to the other side. It is in the air, and they are going to get set to return it if they can. What should you be doing during this long interval besides standing there watching the ball and wondering whether it's going to bounce in or out? Let me make a suggestion. If you are playing the forehand court of your side, and if you have any talent at the net at all, you ought to be advancing to the net. Particularly is this true if the lob is going over to your opponent's backhand, and he has to do considerable moving to get into position. He (or she, of course) may plan to return it with a backhand stroke. This would mean he has failed to make the elementary observation that any reasonably intelligent tennis player should be able to make: that the width of his shoulders is all the additional travel needed to shift to forehand on a high lob. In short, your opponent may commit a favorite blunder, putting together for himself a weak backhand return, giving you a first-class put-away shot at the ball from your net position. Now, as long as you are up there, follow the ball! Plan to cover the whole cockeyed net when your opponent is returning a deep lob from the backhand side. An easy ball from him constitutes a real chance for you, over a wide range, to cover that net.

Perhaps you will argue that by having run up to the net on your forehand side, you placed your partner at a disadvantage. A lob, you point out, is almost certain to come back. It probably will be over your head on your side. Chance it, to get the net opportunity. Sure, he may lob over you. But it is no real trouble for your partner to move toward his forehand, behind you. There is plenty of time on a high lob.

Now that you are up at the net, let me be very controversial. If their lob return is more or less near the center, do not even move from your one-sided position at the net. Let your partner do the moving at the back. In situations where lobs are going back and forth, net players generally shift sides too often. All that oscillating to and fro, left to right, at the net in an attempt to anticipate where the next shot is coming confuses your partner, tires you out, and often really does not change anything in a series of lob returns. You're not going to be handling the lobs; your partner is, and so he still has to shift position with the ball, no matter what you do at the net. In handling the return of a lob from the other side, if you are at the net at all, then choose your location by keeping your purpose in mind. Your purpose is to try to pick off a smash when an error by your opponents gives you a chance at the ball. So watch the ball as they go to hit it. If they botch it so that it is slow and easy, move to clobber

it, disregarding your partner, who is back. He may complain
that he *could* have gotten it had you let it alone, especially if
you spoil it accidentally. But it is right for you to move over
and try to kill an easy one.

Let's consider your partner now. You on the forehand side
have already run up to the net as indicated, your opponent is
receiving a lob, your partner is back over on the backhand
side. What does she do? (Somehow I feel your partner is
a girl.) The answer is, Priscilla should wait for the lob or the
drive, whatever it is, confident there is a good chance that
it will be hit out. If it isn't, she should return again as already
discussed—drive it down the center if both opponents are
back, lob it to the backhand if there is a netman in the situation. Priscilla should not bother about crisscrossing lobs first
to one side, then the other. She should hit the ball back in a
way that will increase her chances of simply getting it in
without giving an easy shot to their net player, favoring each
time the backhand corner of her opponents or that center
shot.

Finally, notice your opponents' habits on lobs. Some people will never return a lob with a lob. Pillsbury, for instance,
hates lobs and hopes they will be declared illegal. Whenever
he gets one he always hits it down, simulating a serve-drive,
often into the net. Pillsbury is not a very strong server, so his
"smashes" of a lob will give you a chance if you're at the
net. Therefore, if you or your partner lobs to Pillsbury, particularly his backhand, then move up. A person receiving a
lob after a bounce, standing behind the base line, who insists
always on driving it but who cannot hit the ball very hard,
is committing a botch that you should take advantage of by
being up at the net. So go to the net and don't worry about
the possibility that you and your partner may be stuck up
there together if he lobs after all. That abandonment of the
rear by your partner is unlikely anyway. Not having read

this book and not being a pro, he will probably hang back expecting to handle the usual good old lob return. Let him have that rather boring duty. You be up there exploiting your opponent's error and making a hero of yourself.

10

Halfway Measures

THE LOCATION ON the tennis court most certain to make evident the mediocrity of an ordinary tennis player is halfway between the net and the base line. By standing in that position you can take the routine matter of returning a perfectly ordinary ball coming from the other side and turn it into a massive challenge. An offering of your opponents coming at ordinary speed and height, which you could angle off for a certain point if at the net, or return in a straightforward way if it were allowed to bounce in the middle of the court and come on back to you near the base line, becomes a problem by virtue of your unfortunate point of action. Suddenly, despite the fact that your opponent has done nothing especially brilliant, you are on the defensive. You find yourself staring at a lost point because of your almost certain ineptness in return, or you set things up for your opponent, who has you at his mercy, to take you on his very next shot.

If you happen to be better equipped than your opponents

in speed, sense of timing, control of the angle of your racket, and ability to follow the ball with your eye for precise co-ordination, the halfway measure may be one that you can exploit despite being a nonchampion in general. It is then a case of your knowing where your skill or mediocrity has its peculiar peaks and valleys, and matching your special strengths and weaknesses against those of the enemies on the other side. But if you are an average player, you should pray that your opponents persist in halfway measures, and you should learn how to take advantage of them. Conversely, you should avoid getting caught in the halfway trap yourself.

In this chapter we are concerned with situations in which the halfway measure is penalizing to the player who indulges in it. However, first we shall point out what is good about that "not up and yet not back" position. In the process of showing why it can sometimes be advantageous, we shall also show why it is especially difficult for the undistinguished player to realize this potential good: If you are standing half-way, then you will be returning most of the balls from your opponent without waiting for a bounce (volleys). This means that when the ball and your racket collide, the ball will be coming at higher speed than if you had taken it after a bounce farther back on the court. It also means that, if hit well, the ball will come off your racket toward your oppo-nent with more speed. It will get back to him in less time, giving him less of an opportunity to judge where you will hit the ball and to get into position to handle it. Thus, if you have sufficient speed in coordination and control of your racket, you have the chance of making faster, better-placed returns that your opponent will be less able to cope with. And, by standing in a halfway position, you will discourage lobs by your opponent as well because, if he attempts one, you might be able with a step or two backward to hit it be-fore it bounces and smash it back for a solid point. Finally, in the event of a slow and weak return from the back courts by your opponents, you can move up to the net for a kill.

These potential advantages of the halfway position are also, however, a foundation for explaining why the mediocre player is usually in trouble in that position. Such a player lacks the speed to be able to respond in the shorter time. He needs the bounce to take some of the steam out of the ball coming to him. By being back, on the other hand, he is able to take more time to choose his position as the ball travels toward him over the longer distance. Handling a ball without the bounce requires a short swing and sometimes even just a blocking action with the racket adjusted so that the angle will be right. The speed of eye and the judging and setting of the relative angles of ball trajectory and racket generally both fall very short of adequate for the average player.

The handling of the ball without a bounce is especially difficult on the backhand side for the less-than-pro player. At least on the forehand the higher balls are somewhere near the region where we are accustomed to position the ball for the serve. It is also tough to block, reflect away, and adjust the position and angle of the racket if the ball comes right at you, rather than to one side or the other, so that you have to have the racket more or less in front of your middle.

The worst shots to handle from a halfway position are the low ones, where your racket has to be held down far from your eyes so that the judging problem for both the position of the racket and for its angle and tilt is, for the ordinary player, a touch of the impossible. The worst situation of all is the ball that bounces a few inches ahead of the racket. It is bad enough to judge the ball down low if it travels one continuous path to your racket, but that last-minute little bounce means a sudden change in the ball's direction and angle to which you must equally suddenly adjust, or which you must sense accurately way ahead of time. There is nothing more difficult in all of tennis. If you can really do this well, picking the ball up off the ground after that sudden, short little bouncing reversal, then you should really consider working hard to bring into your system the rest of what you need to be able to play in a halfway position. You are a candidate for "pro," for eligibility to go after the full exploitation of the advantages, rather than being only a reaper of the disadvantages, of the halfway measures.

So in this chapter we shall cater to the ordinary player who too often finds that when caught halfway he is a sitting duck. There may be beautiful advantages to be gained by operating from that position, but he is not fast enough or coordinated enough to gain them. He merely succeeds, when he stations himself halfway, in raising the level of play, from the standpoint of speed, above his own level. For such players, our discussion boils down to two things. One is, How do you avoid getting into a halfway position? The other is, If you find yourself halfway anyway, how do you get out of that position as quickly as possible, preferably without losing the very next point?

The commonest way imaginable to get into a halfway stance is to start the game that way. We have already said that you should not station yourself there when your partner is serving. Rather, you should move up closer to the net, or in certain special cases discussed earlier, go all the way back to the base line. Moreover, you are not going to be up halfway while you are serving or while you are receiving. Your opponents will not let you in the former instance—they will call that a foot fault—and I hope that your partner or your own good sense will not let you in the second instance.

That leaves only one possibility for your starting the play halfway, which is when your partner is receiving. In fact, it is quite common to start the game in a halfway position (Florsheim in Fig. 47) when your partner (McCoy in Fig. 47) is receiving. The reasoning behind this choice of position

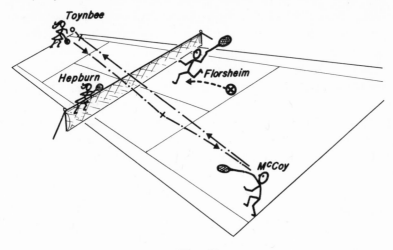

Fig. 47.

for the partner of the receiver leans heavily on the idea of exploiting the advantages of the halfway position. Since Florsheim is not fast enough to take advantage of the opportunities that are supposed to come to someone in that position, we must have some other reasons for his starting there. Let's see what some of these could be. Why should Florsheim, a mediocre player, stand in the vicinity of the service line near the center of the court when the opponents' server, Toynbee, starts serving to his partner, McCoy? One reason could be that McCoy usually displays a strong return of serve. Most of the time he puts it back deep and probably gives the server a rough ball to handle—he never gives a put-away shot to the netman. Under these circumstances, by playing halfway, Florsheim has the time and can be ready to move up to the net for a kill in anticipation of Toynbee's weak return of McCoy's strong ball.

This raises the question: Why should Florsheim not be up at the net in the first place and not take a chance on having to run up? After all, if he is wrong about that expected weak return from Toynbee, and if Toynbee sends it back fast instead, he may catch Florsheim still about halfway with a ball at his feet, just exactly what Florsheim does not want. The answer is that, indeed, Florsheim *has* to be able to get up to the net after the ball is hit by McCoy, if he has that in mind. He must wait to move up until he sees that McCoy has hit the ball well. However, there is always the danger that McCoy may get careless for one play, return poorly, even let the netman Hepburn have a shot at it. Florsheim may not be in too good a position to retrieve the point wherever he is positioned if Hepburn knows what he is doing. But it is utterly out of the question for Florsheim to do anything to help McCoy if Hepburn gets hold of the ball and Florsheim is all the way up to the net. There is at least a little chance that the netman Hepburn, surprised by McCoy's giving him an opportunity, may hit the ball in a mediocre fashion—and Florsheim, playing halfway, will get a real chance to hit it back.

What about the possibility of Florsheim's being able to choose whether to go up or to go back for a lob in case Toynbee decides to lob McCoy's return? There is that option, of course, in theory. But it should be rated as quite secondary. Florsheim's partner, McCoy, can always move over for a high lob, which usually offers plenty of time to do just that. If the lob falls short, Florsheim can return it, if he has not yet run forward. The important thing remains, however, that Florsheim must be able to get up to the net so that he can block a return with a wide-angle shot off to one side, and make the point. That is the commonest follow-up to McCoy's strong return. Remember, it is a lot easier to get your racket in front of the ball to block it and make the point if you are near the net than if you are back away from it by fifteen feet. If Florsheim cannot manage this easily, it is unwise for him to start halfway in the hope of gaining occasional other advantages. In summary, you may start at a halfway position when your partner receives, keeping your eye carefully on their netman until your partner's return has safely passed him; then you should plan to move up to the net. You start watching the server's attempt to get your partner's ball back in order to confirm that you should move up, and to tell you where at the net you should be.

What do you do when your partner is receiving if you expect him to have difficulty with the serve? We assume either that the serve is strong or your partner is weak. Maybe the serve is not extremely strong but just well-positioned—for example, to your partner's backhand, and your partner has difficulty getting a backhand serve back. Should you go ahead with an opening stance in the halfway position, the traditional, international pro position for tennis doubles? Your decision here will depend a great deal on the nature of your partner's difficulty with return of serve and on the ability of the netman on the other side. Let us suppose, for example, that what typically happens is that your partner gives the ball to their netman, who promptly angles it way over to the side and seems to be able to do only that well, rather than position it in general about the court as he chooses. Under such circumstances, you would not want to play all the way back at the base line and be out of the play entirely. You would want to start halfway up and be on your toes, prepared to move either way to try to return that well-angled ball. Of course, if theirs is a really good netman and your partner gives the ball to him to do with as he pleases, it doesn't really matter where you stand. You will look less comical if you do not allow yourself to be an awkward target at whose feet he directs his ball, adding insult, if not injury, to your loss of the point—so you might as well play back or at the net as halfway.

There are some net players who are not particularly versatile and who always do only one thing with an easy ball that comes to them: They simply hit it straight ahead of them, not having the control or the thought process to do any angling of the ball. If that is the kind of netman to whom your partner delivers his returns of serve, you ought to play back. You may well get a chance to do a good drive on his ball, which will be, for all practical purposes, unexceptional, just like any other ball that you might expect to take after a bounce from the back-court position.

This covers the situation of your starting the game in a halfway position. But suppose you find yourself there in the middle of the game? How can that come about, and what do you do about it when it does? Let's eliminate first the one situation over which you have full control—the triple fault of Chapter 2. Running up after an easy serve carries with it the great risk, you will recall, of being caught halfway by the positive and well-hit ball of the receiver. You can stop this by stopping the triple fault. Don't run up after an easy serve.

How about the "medium good" server who runs up to the halfway position? He should do this, obviously, only if he is one of those exceptional players who has the speed to work from that position. He is not the kind of player we are seeking to protect in this chapter.

Most often, perhaps, you find yourself caught halfway after being forced to move up to return a ball. This might occur because of an inadvertently easy shot from the other side, one that just clears the net, bounces, and refuses to come back to you. Or it might be a deliberate "drop" shot by the opponent to take advantage of the fact that you are playing back. The little dump shot of your enemy brings you up, you return it, and there you are, halfway. Another possibility is a poorly executed lob attempt of theirs, or a return by their netman so badly handled that you get a chance at it only if you run up halfway to return it.

In all these instances, that halfway position is one to which you have raced in order to recover the opponent's placement, planned or accidental. You are there, and you can either stay there or get out. If you decide to escape the trap, then you either have to go to the net or run back. Unfortunately, under these circumstances you are usually already on the defensive. You have run hard to get the ball back, and there you are in the halfway spot with little time for contemplation.

Here, we shall simplify our advice. Forget the idea of ever running back. At that instant, there may be something about the game suggesting that you can and should go back to position yourself for what looks like the inevitable return by the opponent. Instinct may cause you to do so during the game. We do not want to fight that instinct. All we mean is this: Have in mind, when you run up to recover a short ball and get stuck halfway, that you ought to consider going all the way or staying where you are, but not going back. If you have got up to the halfway point and returned the ball for which you had to run—returned it well so that it is going to be taken by the opponents in their back court and not by their netman—then by all means continue to go forward. Your opponent will not only need to get adjusted to the fact that you ran and successfully handled his short shot, but to a new net situation as well. He is not Rosewall, and he cannot readily handle such rapidly developing multiple situations on the other side of the net from him. If, on the other hand, you have not returned well and your shot is going to be handled by their side up short, you are better off to stay where you are and take your chances on being embarrassed by a shot at your feet. Who knows—he may give you an easy one that you can handle from there. If you try to get all the way back near your back line, your slowness in retreating will mean that you will not be there soon enough to get a good, strong stance even if the ball does arrive there. On the other hand, should you have to handle another short one, either because he is clever or because he is exercising the full privileges of mediocrity, you will not return from the rear in time to care for it. So advance forward or stay halfway on short plays; don't retreat.

We should close this discussion of halfway measures by pointing out that rules, including those in this chapter, can sometimes do you in. You must watch the particular strong characteristics of mediocrity in your opponents in order to know where you had best stand. One young lady I know always returns a serve with a short one over the net. She seems unable to do anything else. For her, the server would do well to run up halfway, that being just the right position to hit the ball back firmly and strongly to her backhand, which she always misses. But remember, a halfway measure can be very costly. Don't just repeatedly and absentmindedly resort to it. Think it out carefully.

11

Botches and Sons of Botches

If YOU ARE eminently eligible to be a reader of this textbook, you are a player of tennis who is destined to be below champion caliber no matter how hard you try, because you lack one or another important talent or ability that will enable you, even if you work zealously, to elevate yourself to that category. However, the purpose of this book is to improve your ability to win and, on the assumption that that is what you wish you could do some of the time at least, thus to increase your enjoyment of the game. In this chapter, we want to consider a series of blunders that you probably commit your share of, more than occasionally. If you are quite often guilty of most of the major botches described here, then you qualify for a somewhat more exclusive category of individuals—those who are both mediocre and idiotic; but we hope to help you overcome these bad habits that cost you so dearly in points and in satisfaction.

Let's be certain what we mean by a botch. If you are a little tired, or a little slow even when fresh, and the opponents are pushing you around with higher speed than you can counter, with better placed balls than you can recover; or if you occasionally hit the ball out or into the net on a perfectly ordinary play; or if your backhand is weaker than your forehand, and your serve is often too easy; or if you let your racket slip and take your eyes off the ball occasionally—these things merely prove that you are average. When you are caught in one of these situations and lose the point, we would not define that as a botch. Such a failure is regrettable, it is costly, but it is part of your lower level of play.

A botch is something else again. It is a type of error, a mess, in which you cannot in any way blame the performance of your opponents or of your partner. A botch has to be an act that you do entirely on your own. Furthermore, it has to be something that is unnecessary, that results not from your limited ability to play the game of tennis in the physical sense, but rather from your shortcomings in the thinking department. You have to lose the point in an inexcusable way to create a botch. You have to take a ball from your opponent that is quite returnable within the scope of your abilities, and then manage somehow—not occasionally, but quite often —to lose the point. You have to do it all out of your own little head, or by default in the use of your head, rather than by your lack of speed or agility. *That* is a botch.

In addition to the botch, there is the S.O.B., the "son of a botch." This, as the name implies, is a second-generation botch, the consequence of an earlier botch. An S.O.B. is a lost point that embarrasses you and makes your opponents happy as a result of the way your earlier botch set up the situation against yourself. Most mediocre players fail to appreciate properly the botch that is really responsible for the son of a botch. They focus attention only on the S.O.B.'s that lose the points—just as we frequently blame the kids when it is what the parents did a generation before that caused the kids to go wrong. Sons of botches are even more costly over a period of time than their parental botches—for many reasons.

For one thing, as is customary for second generations of offspring, there may be two S.O.B.'s or more for every botch. Now I know you can lose only one point at a time, but you can so mess up your game with a botch that you and your partner are exhausted and throw away a lot of easy ones for a whole game or two as a result. You can set up a whole series of generations of botches to follow the original one. You can be so disgusted with yourself, or your partner can be so disgusted with you, that both your teamwork and individual confidence will be shattered for many points after the original botch. Tragic next-generation effects result from unplanned parenthood in botchery. You can even commit a botch without noticing it, and such a botch can later yield its inevitable bad result, altering your strategy for the worse in the game that follows, setting off a series of other drastic mistakes, which are properly called sons and grandsons of botches.

Perhaps the most common botch repeatedly achieved by the mediocre player is directing an easy serve into the net. My careful statistical research into this interesting but disturbing phenomenon shows that, for the typical set of ten games in which the server of each game offers an average of seven or eight serves that have to be returned, half are readily returnable, and half of those are directed into the net by the mediocre receiver. The analysis of numerous matches with many mediocre players who persist in this habit has resulted in the accompanying table listing, in order of frequency, the most common reasons for hitting the ball into the net. It must be emphasized that until these definitive researches were performed, most dilettante observers of the "easy-serve-return-into-the-net" phenomenon assumed that it was due either to something mysteriously tricky about the serve or something inherently lacking in the capability of the receiver. A study of the table shows that the true reasons lie entirely in the category of curable mental conditions not really related to the inherent capability of the mediocre player as an athlete.

TABLE OF
INTO-THE-NET BOTCHES

a. Talking
b. Not ready
c. Not expecting the first serve to be in
d. Racket suddenly let loose at the instant of hitting the ball
e. Still deciding whether to take the ball forehand or back-backhand, after it has been returned
f. Standing in a very bad place for that particular server's approach to serving
g. Trying to kill a low bouncer

It is clear that, to cure persistent and insistent delivery of the ball into the net on an easy serve, you have first of all to recognize that you are a victim of this particular malady and that it is a mental problem. You will never get anywhere unless you are willing to acknowledge that you have this addiction problem. Next time you play three sets, try, just for the heck of it, to make a mental note of how often you hit an easy serve into the net. If you do it around ten times in a morning of three sets, you are very close to needing help, which only you yourself can provide, starting with the firm conviction that something has to be done.

Of course, the table covers only the most common reasons, averaging the characteristics of a large number of individuals. Many creatively mediocre players have unique pet habits that no one else has, which manifest themselves in this tendency to botch. Your particular problem may simply be over-excitement as a result of a brilliant point that you just scored. This is known as the "inverted son of a botch" effect, or the "reciprocated anti-botch." Here is the way it works: A superb display of superior tennis on your part, something you are not used to, produces second- and third-generation pseudogenetic effects on your performance for several points thereafter. The more unlikely and outstanding and highly applauded your occasional good shot that wins a colorful point, the longer you commit botches in all the following plays before your system recovers—clearly a mental problem.

You may have to do a little research of your own, but try the table anyway. For one thing, stop talking anywhere near the period of time in which the serve is being delivered to you. Expect the first one to go in, and be just as ready for it as you are for the second one. Hold your racket loose on the way to the court but quit doing so when you are about to hit the ball. Choose a sensible place to stand by making a deliberate effort to figure out your position ahead of time. In this regard, you should notice what the server does to your partner as well as to you, and try to accumulate a little calibrated experience with regard to that server. After having chosen your position, you should settle in your mind the general area that you will think of as requiring a backhand and the general area that requires a forehand. If, because of a severe spin, the server fools you the first time or so, then start taking that into account. Deliberately and determinedly, be thinking all the time. If he still goes on fooling you, then at least what you do in failing to return cannot be called a botch.

It is especially tempting to hit an easy serve hard, overlooking the fact that by the time you hit it, the ball may not be very high. In fact, the height of the ball when the racket connects with it may be much below the net. You must get into the habit of bending your knees, getting under the ball, and concentrating on getting it over the net, hopefully not a lot over, but at least over. Hitting the ball hard is for a harder serve or a higher-bounce kind of easy serve, or for one you connect with farther back so that you *can* hit it hard, clear the net, and still not go over the back line.

At this point we should mention that a common reason for hitting the net on some easy serves is that they are low and you have to lift them, and being a mediocre receiver, in hitting them up you very often go right over the back line without realizing that you are swinging so freely. Then, next in trying to keep from being long on your return, you start aiming the ball lower and it collides with the net. Some mediocre receivers have been known to respond to the easy serve for several sets, one after the other, by oscillating with regularity between favoring the net on one return and driving to the back court on the next. There must be a place in between, and a mediocre player capable of both testing the net and perfecting the long and out shot should have a reasonable chance of getting the ball in between occasionally. This should happen even if he does not think about it, and if he keeps thinking about it, it ought to be very much easier to get the ball just in between. But he has to have at least the interest and the perception to notice that he *is* hitting the net or hitting the ball long as often as he is. Some mediocre players seem not to notice what they are doing. They have the vague impression they are losing the game because of something their partners do or because the opponents are generally superior. If they are superior, it is only because of unnecessary and curable stupidity on the part of the mediocre receiver.

In leaving return of serve and going to other common botches, those inexcusable independent actions of a mediocre player that lose him points without any requirement for competence on the part of his opponents, we shall test a number of them with less depth. The general idea will probably be clear without our belaboring each problem. After all, we have been discussing botches in all the text so far, and here we propose only to complete the discussion by pointing out some important ones not previously mentioned.

An excellent and conspicuous botch results when your

opposition has gotten themselves discombobulated in their positions and, with the whole court available to you to return an easy ball from them, you nevertheless deliver it right to their netman's ready racket. He is surprised, having virtually given up the point because of his awkward location and not readily imagining you would be so imbecilic. But he is not so surprised that he is unable to capitalize on the wonderful opportunity you have given him. Why do some mediocre players persist in setting up the ball for the netman on the other side when they are not on the defensive themselves and could just as well put the ball elsewhere? It seems to be some sort of temporary aphasia, lapse of the ability to think, a temporary confusion as to what the game is. My own theory is that it goes back to the player's babyhood—to "patty-cake," or the first throwing of a soft ball to daddy. After all, we all played "catch" before we played tennis. We played cooperative baby games before competitive ones. The idea of getting the ball to the other fellow so that he can handle it easily was strongly imprinted on our brains as infants. The deep and controlling pattern of thought is there in your brain. All you have to do is get excited, or let your attention lapse a little bit, or lose your concentration in a game, and you revert to this infantile thought pattern programmed so early and solidly in your mind. That's my theory. The answer is to pay attention (and also, grow up).

Many mediocre players suffer from an emotional thought-process problem, which has its sources, I am sure, not in early childhood, but in the earlier stages of precivilized man. I refer to the desire to kill. Players manifest this on the tennis court by their complete loss of sensible control when a great and glorious opportunity suddenly is presented to them. For instance, your two opponents may have returned a fairly straightforward ball to you, and through some sort of mix-up clearly left most of the court completely undefended. This may have occurred because a net player became confused, raced to get the ball, missed it, passed it, found himself way over at the alley at one side while his partner ran to get behind that ball on the same side back in the corner. The ball they somehow return to you is a high bouncer, and so located that you could step up leisurely and hit it while standing in about the middle of your court. You could clear the net very easily, hit it overhand or at your side, as you choose, to almost anywhere in the two-thirds of the court they have left open. You know it, they know it, your partner knows it. Sometimes the situation is made even more interesting psychologically because your two opponents, in the confusion, both turn and race to the extreme other side so that they are really nowhere, just busy running frantically. Then you not only have the two-thirds of the court they vacated, but can even put the ball where they are—and there is nothing that they are ready to do. Remember—everybody knows this, including you. It's a cinch point, a gorgeous opportunity, a gift.

But you want more than just the point. At least, that part of your brain that suddenly takes over wants more. It wants blood. And so you go all-out to show how hard you can hit the ball, and how extreme an angle you can introduce into your return. But why don't you just return the ball in a straightforward way and make the point? You don't and you can't. The result is that you hit out or into the net. Your humiliation and ruined morale and your partner's unavoidable and conspicuously noticeable disgust are matched only by the tremendous boldness of confidence created in your opponents. Because they now think somebody up there likes them. They see they were apparently protected against your killer instinct by a higher force, one that presumably stands ready to do it again and will back them up for the rest of the day. So this is not only a botch. It is botch that produces a whole family of sons and grandsons. I have known this kind of thing to upset a mediocre player not only for the match or the day, but for several business deals in the following months.

There is a hypnotic botch that sometimes takes control of a so-so player who gets into a long rally with a so-so player on the other side, each of whom is proud of his particular shot, such as a cross-court forehand. Thus, you have Jonathan, deep in his forehand court, hitting the ball deep to the forehand court of Von Luger, who returns it deep to the forehand court of Jonathan. Back and forth they go, challenged by the necessity for continued power and control and steadiness. All the while Jonathan seems not to have noticed that Von Luger's partner, Clay, a substantially weaker player with a weak backhand, is standing back at the base line, out of shape because he has not had a ball for some time. Why doesn't Jonathan occasionally place one of those balls to Clay, straight along, parallel to the alley, to Clay's backhand. It is a straightforward shot that does not involve any more risk than continuing to return the ball to Von Luger's forehand. It is a botch not to do so, particularly if Jonathan has a netman, Stassen, not much worse than the others, who is standing near the net where he might put away Clay's weak return.

Indeed, this is a case where there are several good alternatives. We really ought to consider that Jonathan is committing many botches as he persists in overlooking all the other desirable routes. For example, he can direct the ball right between Clay and Von Luger so that Von Luger has to take it on his backhand and may run into conflict with partner Clay, who thinks he should be returning that same center shot with his forehand.

But no, Jonathan is hypnotized by the back-and-forth operation in which he is engaged. He can no longer think. His total mental capacity is set on ensuring that he will not miss before Von Luger does. Maybe he will even make it. Maybe Von Luger *will* finally miss a ball before Jonathan. Then,

Jonathan will think, we cannot charge him with a botch. Maybe not, but we can charge him with some sons of botches because being an ordinary player, Jonathan will be tired out from all that exercise. He will also have the wrong impression that this procedure is what he ought to follow. So he will play that way against everyone, including the player who is just a shade steadier, and will lose points. This is a shame because he could easily hit the ball to one of the two other places, not to mention combinations of drop shots and other changes of pace to change the setup.

In general, it has got to be considered a botch to play the ball without continually having in mind which of the opposing two players had best be given a chance for error in handling the regular, ordinary ground shots during the course of the play.

Some of the many botches inherent in what has been discussed earlier in this text are worth listing here in a slightly different way. It is a botch when you are up by the net during the course of play (whether you started there or have shifted your position to that region) if you do not guard your alley as the first priority whenever your partner has hit an easy one to an opponent who at that moment happens to be lined up along that alley for the return. It is equally a botch at the net not to be moving with the ball. Specifically, in your net position you should be willing to move away more from the alley toward the center if you note that your partner's ball or serve is bouncing closer to the center of the court.

There is a type of overconscientiousness afflicting some players that shows up conspicuously when they are at the net. They are anxious to play all balls that come near them, and are somewhat more embarrassed than they need to be if a ball gets by them. In this habit of overregretting, they fail to discriminate between the balls that get by them at the net on their alley side, which cannot be handled by their partner, and those on the other (center) side of them that their partner might cover. Of course there are balls that it would be almost a miracle if the netman's partner were able to get his racket on. (Balls that go over the net player's head, that are lobs or nearly so, give the partner—we are assuming that he is back, although over in the other court—at least a fighting chance to get there. We are not talking about those now.) How much to regret a ball that has passed you at the net or anywhere else does not interest us. We are discussing common botches. The common botch we are now getting at is the situation in which a low and perhaps easy one has escaped you on the center-court side. It is on its way to your partner, who will return it in a moment—if you leave it alone. But you simply can't leave it alone. It is past you; you cannot hit it well. In fact, if it really bounces past your feet, you cannot hit it at all except sideways and back, rather than toward your opponents. In other words, what you succeed in doing by your stubbornness in trying to hold onto the ball, as though there were an award for touching it is merely to tick it with the edge of your racket, to ruin it for your partner, and to lose the point.

12

Divorce, Tennis Style

WE HAVE INSISTED throughout the text that ordinary tennis players should play doubles. The areas to be covered in singles are unsuited to the scope of coverage and control of the players. Singles is all right as a practice opportunity to prepare for the real game of nonpro tennis, which is doubles. A good singles match, satisfying to both sides, needs to be played in accordance with the concepts of pro tennis. To superimpose upon a singles match—where each player is intent, and has to be, on the pro objective of hitting the ball so hard and/or placing it so well that his opponent will be unable to return it, or will return a ball that is an easy put-away—the abundance of straight-and-out errors that characterizes the average player's game is simply not sound. A book of this kind, dealing as it does exclusively in irreproachable principles, simply cannot discuss a game that bypasses all logic.

But there is one fundamental problem with which we must

deal in average tennis the moment we insist that it always be doubles: Each player must have a partner. This introduces a specific human element different from any in tennis singles. It is a problem not exclusive to tennis, but that occurs quite frequently in our social system, often under the common title of "marriage."

There has to be a basis of cooperation and compatibility between two tennis partners attempting to divide the errors of tennis between them. After all, you cannot both hit the same arriving ball into the net, although each of you can try. And you have to take turns receiving and serving, although who goes first and who stands on which side is sometimes a severe problem. If you cannot get these things worked out so that you share happiness rather than distress most of the time, then you and your partner probably need a divorce. Just as it has now been established that you do not have to be Jewish, or even a mother, to be a Jewish mother, so you do not have to be married to your tennis partner in order to require a divorce on grounds of incompatibility, cruelty, neglect, or consorting (in this case with the enemy, and inadvertently).

In this chapter, we shall attempt to deal with several things related to this partnership. We shall try for a good marriage. Then, on the assumption that things may not go well, we shall offer some counseling in the hope that you may be able to save something out of all that you and your partner have built up together. Finally, we will take a strong stand for divorce as a last-resort way out when needed. If the principles of this chapter are followed, you may even be able to play tennis with your real-life spouse as your partner with few bad effects, although it is more likely that, if married, you will enhance your chances of remaining so by avoiding playing as tennis partners. Yet I know one couple who got a divorce in real life and are now very happy and compatible as tennis partners. Actually, these two individuals are not mediocre tennis players; they happen to be pros, as we have defined the term. What they were—well, they were mediocre husband and wife.

It is characteristic of pro-type players that they tend to choose their tennis partners with considerable care—even for fun matches, not just for tournament play. Mediocre players go out on the court, four of them, and are very likely to team up according to some completely irrelevant social pairing, or just at random.

The first step here is an exception to the conclusion we have usually come to in this book. This time, follow the pros. Think in terms of selecting partners who will supplement each other and compensate for each other's weaknesses. Since you want to enjoy the game, you should choose a partner so that those aspects of the game from which each of you derives his greatest satisfaction will not be precluded and circumvented by the pattern of play of the other—with whom it is necessary to get along and share errors.

First, however, let us talk about the basic personality part of overall compatibility. (We'll defer the direct matter of dividing up fairly between you the creating of botches or, rather, trying to ensure that the opponents on the other side of the net make even more errors than you.) For a tennis partner, you should select a person who is mature and has a fine personality. The accompanying table will be helpful in making your choice. It lists the minimum requirements your partner should meet.

PERSONALITY TABLE
CRITERIA FOR PARTNER'S PERSONALITY

He should be:

Considerate
Tactful
Understanding

Respectful
Sympathetic
Able and willing to tell little white lies
Calm
Courageous
Appreciative
Possessed of high morale
Possessed of sense of humor
A leader (though sometimes a follower)
Cooperative
Self-sacrificing
Intelligent
Adaptable
Willing
Trustworthy
Generous
Good

If you examine this table, you will see that there will be no problem in finding any number of friends who have all the personality and character traits listed. The problem is, do you have them? Fortunately, it is you who is reading this text. So we need only give you some helpful hints that will make you appear to your potential partners to have a personality integrating the criteria listed in the table. For this purpose, we have accumulated a group of "don'ts." Just refrain from doing the things that we label "out," and you too can be a partner whose personality, at least, provides a basis for a good court marriage. (I was going to say "courtship," but that would really make this text mediocre, wouldn't it?)

Naturally, you do not regularly do each and every one of the things we are going to describe, but there are plenty of others that you do frequently that should be entered as additional "don'ts." This list of "don'ts" evolved from researches covering many, many matches, over a period of many years, in all parts of the country. We discovered so many hundreds of common, personality-impairing habits of mediocre players that we cannot mention them all. Set down here are only those most frequently observed, which were also seen to be the most penalizing in the maintenance of a good partner-to-partner relationship.

Don't keep saying, "sorry, sorry, sorry, nuts, doggone it," and so on, every time you miss a shot. You do not owe your partner an apology unless he was denied his rightful opportunity to miss the same shot, on account of what you did. Spare him the monotony and drudgery of listening to your patter. It is bad enough that you keep ruining the points.

Don't tell your partner that he has to get the next point: "It's forty-love. You have to return his serve this time or we've lost the game!" He knows it. He may be only average like you, but he remembers that if he does not make the point he will lose it. He might even have made it if you had not raised his annoyance quotient. Most mediocre receivers of service, immediately following an insult, hit the ball into the net.

Don't make suggestions about how to play. If he insists on your doing so—he honors you by feeling you can help him with your comments—make them after the game, never during it. First of all, it is presumptuous on your part; your suggestion may not be so smart. Maybe what he is doing is better, and you are simply too lacking in perception or understanding to realize that. Perhaps what he will try is the best thing for him to do, even though it might not be what you would do under the same circumstances. Remember, each of you is so-so in some respects in his own way, even if well above average in other respects.

Don't keep saying, "Good shot," or "Good serve," to congratulate your surprised opponent whenever you miss a perfectly easy one he has just sent you. Whom do you think you're kidding?

Never, never demand an explanation: "Why didn't you hit it to his backhand corner?" All such demands for explanation are silly questions for at least three reasons: 1) You may very well have the wrong idea—the backhand corner was not the right place; the alley shot he chose was right. Just because he happened to miss does not prove it was not the correct play. 2) He had no choice. He barely got his racket on the ball. He is not that fast or strong or coordinated. 3) He is stupid, that's why; what good does it do to ask for an explanation when that is the answer?

Be careful when you yell, "It's yours." The time to do that is when you definitely cannot get it, and you hope he will rescue you even though that might require some magic. He will forgive you and laugh it off if it is utterly and noticeably absurd. A typical wrong time to call "It's yours" is when he stands poised to do something useful with a fairly straightforward ball being delivered to him, and you are nowhere near. Then your "It's yours" can only be interpreted by him to mean that you are expecting something extra of his performance on that shot. So he just has to hit it out or into the net—you have upset his normal play.

Don't talk, squeal, scream, giggle, groan, or sigh while your partner is receiving or serving, or at any time during the play. Tennis, even mediocre tennis, is not square dancing. Your motions and those of other players need no verbal accompaniment to stay in rhythm.

Use directions sparingly. "Run up," "Out," and "Stay" had better be right, good, clear, and prompt, or else you are simply a doggone nuisance.

Don't shift to a completely different position at the net as he goes to throw the ball up for his serve. Don't run behind him to back him up every time he moves to the net—especially if he is back to return a lob.

Don't comment on every play or analyze what happened. If you care that much about it, write up notes at home and present a term paper occasionally, or write a book like this. But keep it off the court.

Don't explain why you missed a ball. So you lifted an easy high one to the netman, who put it away for a lovely point. Why tell everyone that you planned to put it over his head? They know you were trying to make a point rather than to lose it. The momentarily interesting thing is that you failed. They learned that when you did it. It's already old stuff when you start your explanation.

Don't say, "I thought I'd test you," or "I thought you were asleep," to their netman after giving him a put-away shot that you shouldn't have. It may please your opponent to know that he fooled you, but it also gripes the heck out of your partner.

The foregoing are samples. I suggest you add a few of your own favorites. A lot of these "don'ts," which are based on personality traits you possess as a potential partner, are annoying to your opponents as well as to your partner. Cut them out, or you may need a divorce from the whole shebang.

Since we are all human, none of us will have a high score on all the traits in the list. And we will, from time to time, indulge in the forbidden don'ts. Our departure from perfection will be more and more frequent as we feel the strain, and strain can come from poor teamwork. Poor teamwork, in turn, can result with partners of the highest motivation and personal maturity and charm if the "teaming up" is not good. The worst teaming-up comes from mismatching the strengths and weaknesses of the two partners. If they don't line up properly to compensate for and support each other, both are frustrated and neither can perform well as a person or as a tennis player.

Consider an example of an unfortunate wedding between two perfectly good, reliable, ordinary players with fine personalities, Axelrod and Wheeling. Axelrod is a bit below the average of the four players who have come together, in the general departments that make up overall play—with one sparkling exception. At the net he is very quick with eye and arm, and accurate. Wheeling, on the other hand, is a bit better than average in general, with one weakness that is quite conspicuous. His serve is easier than that of the three others, and though it cannot be killed, it can be returned firmly to wherever the receiver desires.

Team these attractive gentlemen, and poor Axelrod gets little chance throughout the entire afternoon to put his great net talent to work. He never gets to handle balls at the net when his partner is serving. The serve is hit so readily by the receiver, who moves up on it, that Axelrod becomes a kind of target. Or, equally frustrating, the serve is always returned away from the net player, as the receiver chooses. Axelrod even considers playing back on Wheeling's serve to avoid embarrassment, since his net-play is made to look poor or useless, and he is concerned and embarrassed about having a bad day. The fault really lies with Wheeling's poor serve. When Axelrod does move back, Wheeling is a bit put out, which does not make Axelrod feel any better either.

But the situation is even worse than this. For the rest of the play, as we said, Axelrod is a little bit below par. Thus, Wheeling finds that his generally above-average play (except for his serve) is quite often frustrated by the higher-than-average number of errors made by his partner Axelrod. Clearly, Axelrod should look for a partner who has the best serve of the group, even if that player is poor in other respects. Then he would get a chance to be a hero with his net-play.

Another example will suffice. Sears is a lob artist, both in delivery and in receiving. That is, he likes to take the serve from the other side and lob it over the opposing netman's head. He also likes to play back, to handle high ones after the bounce. For some reason or other, Sears does not like the net. He prefers to stay away from it and to keep it out of the play entirely. There are a lot of people like that. For instance, there is Roebuck. Roebuck is exactly like Sears. But when they team up, then amusing things happen, or sad ones, depending upon which side of the net you are on as you watch them happen.

Whenever Sears is at the net and a lob comes over his head, he always can be counted on to run back to try to get a crack at it—any excuse to leave the net area. The same thought occurs to Roebuck, standing, as he is, over in the other corner. The result is that both Sears and Roebuck go for the same corner together, interfering with each other, trying to get the same ball. This is clearly a double botch because, even if one gets it, they have set up an S.O.B. The return by the other side will be to some area other than their commonly occupied corner, from which they both may be found running at the same time, to about the same other place.

Can you imagine what happens when you get Sears and Roebuck on one side and Montgomery and Ward, who are almost identical in their habits, on the other? The serve is returned by a lob over the netman, with the netman and server both headed for the same corner to get it. Let's assume they do. One of them hits a return lob back to the center, and now Sears and Roebuck have a little contest to see which one will handle it. They are both there. And if one of them does get it back, he lobs it again to the other corner, to which both Montgomery and Ward now race. We end our example here. May the best combine win.

An embarrassingly obvious point requires discussion here principally because it is the best possible example of misplaced courtesy, false modesty, and thoughtlessness, all mixed up together to attain what is, half the time, a poor decision. This is the question of which partner will choose the backhand and which the forehand court. The opportunities for mismatch here are quite evident.

Take the case of Hopewell and Littlejohn. Both these two average male players play most often in mixed doubles with their wives. For reasons that are more social than logical, each then always plays the backhand court. Thus, year in and year out, they receive most serves to their backhand, and so they finally become fairly reliable at hitting that backhand in a cross-court return that avoids the netman. Now, in the team-up for their occasional men's doubles, each foolishly indicates that he is quite flexible and can play either court. The fact is, neither is any good at playing the forehand court because he is so set in stance and swing for the other court. This is the way it will go: The opponents will serve to Hopewell's backhand. He, being accustomed to hitting a backhand over to his right, will be inclined to do so still despite his unfamiliar new location. A habit is hard to break. But, unfortunately, directing his return to the right is no longer a cross-court. It goes instead to the opposing netman, or wide, for a lost point.

Hopewell and Littlejohn should each choose as a partner someone who prefers the forehand court. Or at least each should recognize the problem so that he and his potential partner can figure out which of them can more easily adjust to the bad situation. Each should speak up and say, "It is much better for me to play the backhand court. That's where I always play, and I know the way home from there."

13

It's All Relative

Since this is a scientific treatise intended as more than merely a tribute to the reader's advance above mediocrity, a final chapter is necessary to make a critical point. We need to restore to scientific purity any oversimplifications or exaggerations that we may inadvertently have made in the preceding chapters, or that we may have chosen as an easy route to elucidating the particular issues under discussion. We make it all up now by borrowing from the man who was probably the supreme scientist of the last century, Albert Einstein.

All that has been said earlier needs to be summarized, and in part reconsidered and amended, to allow for the effect of "relativity." The advice that we have offered and the reasoning on which it was based may often have sounded more absolute than relative. We now wish to recognize that perhaps, relative to your opponent, you are sometimes the equivalent of a pro. Conversely, relative to your opponents, on occasion you may be reduced on individual plays to a degree of helplessness that makes the happy incompetent who faces you a pro—relatively speaking, that is.

Let's quickly run through some of our major conclusions from this relativistic point of view, and see where as a final touch we need to perfect the attainment of a superb ex-ordinary game.

In the first chapter we urged a substantial warm-up period, something we claimed the typical nonpro player was reluctant to engage in. However, if you observe that your opponents (but not your partner!) are wildly erratic during the initial warm-up, so much so that your error rate is relatively small, you should consider a deviation from the warm-up practice we recommended. After all, there is no use in tiring yourself out in a warm-up. It is not so much warming up that you wish to accomplish in that preplay phase. Rather, it is that you want to be more warmed up than your opponent. In effect, then, take temperature readings as you hit the ball back and forth. If you are relatively in better shape than the other side, it is time for you to suggest the start of play.

To move on—earlier, in our analysis of the triple fault, we urged you not to run up to the net after your only modestly effective serve. On an absolute basis—considering the weakness of your serve, your low top speed in running, your limited coordination, your slight ability to respond from a halfway position—this is generally good advice. But let us say you observe that to your opponent, the receiver, your serve apparently presents mysteries and challenges. It seems to push him or her to the limits of capability. In this situation you might consider amending the triple-fault discussion slightly. Observe carefully whether the return is in the blooper, soft, short category. If it is, your speed, coordination, and so on (relatively speaking) may be quite adequate for you to leap forward and put the ball away. Your rush to net may be, in the absolute sense, pretty feeble, yet you will still accomplish the task of hitting the return well, for it all depends upon your relative performance.

In a similar way, when we urged you to play somewhat closer to the net than is the pro's typical position, it was because we wanted to make it easier for you to smash the ball down and away for a sure point when the opportunity came your way. Also, we wanted you to get used to giving up useless attempts to run quickly behind yourself in an effort to cover broad territory, as a champion does, to return a lob that goes over your head. This is, on the average and on an absolute measuring scale, good advice for the mediocre player. Again, however, it is all relative. If the opponent whom you face demonstrates that his return is always of the soft, slow, high type—giving you plenty of time to get your legs, elbows, eyes, etc., set for a good shot—then you can choose a position somewhat farther back from the net. There will be plenty of time, even for you, to lunge forward to slam the shot away as though you had been up close to the net all the while. But you must remember to move forward when you should, or back when you should. Don't just stand there and wait for that slow, uneasy ball being sent toward you to arrive precisely where you are. Einstein wouldn't like it; he would say it violates the law of probability.

If you look back at the chapters on net nettling and net nonsense and non-stance, you will note that we were careful to keep you from extending yourself overambitiously, drifting too far away from the position where you might expect most often to do the most good offensively and defensively. But if your opponent is slow and weak enough, you can at the net virtually cover the entire width of the doubles court. You should consider moving to put the ball away the moment it leaves your opponent's racket. Poaching is, in other words, a relative term and not an absolute one. Your partner will forgive any kind of poach if you make the point. And you *can* make the point at the net against a very feeble adagio return. You can see the ball coming for a long time. Your speed is thus relatively adequate to get you to a good position, with your body and racket squared away, and make it possible for you to angle the ball off for a point.

Some people simply should not play net at all. Their reactions are so slow-motionish, relative to the minimum speed requirements, that all they succeed in doing at the net is troubling themselves a little, disturbing their rest, whenever a ball comes near them. If you face such an opponent (one who really makes you look agile), consider him a perfect target—not to hit purposely, of course (let his partner do that). But give him every opportunity to hand you a point. Hence, in all the conclusions we reached about the important return of serve, you should amend our absolute reasonings in order to deliver the ball to that attractive, bungling netman. This is an extreme case, of course, and one that you must constantly review during the game. I have seen even the most inept netmen, including some whose minds and bodies are ideally mismatched to tennis in its entirety, who, when given enough successive easy balls to return at the net, eventually start connecting with them. They may hit the ball on the wood at first, which will make it even more difficult for you to return. Under these circumstances, you will have gone beyond the proper application of the theory of relativity.

Even our "alternation-lob syndrome" discussion needs a slight relativistic polish to shine with the brightest scientific luster. You will face some opponents for whom one cycle or two of the alternation is sufficient for them to become so confused as to guarantee you the point. It would be a shame not to indulge in repeated lobs and encourage the certain and early errors from them.

Continuing with our relativistic amendments, we should reexamine halfway measures—operating neither at the net or back line, a practice we discouraged before. Playing halfway will not, against a relatively more hopeless player than yourself, guarantee that you will be embarrassed by fast balls at your feet or low ones to either side, as we emphasized so strongly earlier. It may be that, on a relative basis, your opponent can operate only with a short court. That is, he is so poorly adjusted to tennis that he cannot successfully get balls deep into your court, and when he tries, they always go way long. For such an opponent you will have to pretend that the entire court is shorter, and move forward so that you can be ready for his short ones that bounce near the net. You can be confident that you will rarely be caught by one that goes by you and lands in the court you have left behind. Furthermore, the speed of his balls may be so low that you can hit volleys in return, even moving to your left or right or reaching up for them. His actions will be, relative to yours, a sort of man-in-his-sleep exercise. You will look then like a pro, up there halfway.

Unlike the advice given earlier, when you return the blooper serve of a much inferior opponent, you may be justified in staying in the more or less halfway position to which the proper return of his serve has forced you. Your return should be relatively fast, affording him a more than ordinary opportunity to give you another blooper in response, including some balls that will not even get back to you if you retreat to the rear.

Dare we bring the relativistic concept even into the matter of getting along with your partner? Is it all right on some occasions, in accordance with relativity principles, to be obnoxious, to instruct and criticize your partner, to engage in all those annoying habits of yours that would ordinarily destroy your partner's play? The answer is No. Even in Einstein's Theory of Relativity there is one thing that is absolute. Mass, time, length, momentum, general physical measurements, all these are relative and depend upon the observer's environment relative to what he is viewing. But Einstein said that the velocity of light remains a constant, the same to all observers regardless of their relatively different circumstances. Courtesy is to tennis as the velocity of light is to physics, a universal constant. What is good enough for Einstein is good enough for you. Avoid any deviations from the absolute rules laid down on how to stay happily married to your partner.

However, there is another whole side to our relativistic reasoning, corollary to everything discussed so far in this chapter—namely, the relatively inverse situation. What if you find yourself in a game where, compared with you, the other players seem like pros? This can be true of your opponents, of your partner, or of the entire trio. Now, what do you do? To what extent must we embellish or modify what has been said in this book, for this relatively unfortunate situation in which you find yourself?

The easiest circumstance to discuss is the one where you happen to have an exceptionally strong partner. He makes you seem even more incompetent than you are, by the comparison of your contributions with his. This threatens to make you an unhappy incompetent. The answer is to get happier but no more incompetent—a bit of having your cake and eating it too. Here is how. All you have to do is modify your performance on the court to leave as much room and as many of the balls for your partner to handle as possible. When he serves, favor your alley very distinctly, leaving most of the court to him. When he receives a serve, think of the center of the court as his and try to play only your extreme side. You might even consider going up close to the net, hugging your alley as well, so that you can catch and put away an easy reflection of his very good return, and that only. When you receive, plan to leave the middle to him when your returned ball comes back. If you are relatively fast but otherwise quite inept compared with him, you might consider running up to the net (on your alley side, of course) at the flimsiest opportunity and on the least defensible pretense. This will get you out of his way and let him virtually play singles. It is most convenient to run for the net to do this. Do not run off the playing part of the court into the corner; that is being obvious.

What now of the case in which both your opponents are, relatively speaking, champion athletes compared with you? If your partner is in their class, or anyway a lot better than you are, what we have just been saying applies: Arrange to put the main burden on him. If your partner is as bad as you are, clearly we have nothing to add here that has not already been covered in our chapter on divorce. You have teamed up in the wrong way. Get by the first set as best you can, six-love or six-one. Take advantage of the hopelessness of the situation by practicing some overhead smashes or something of that kind. Then, the moment you lose the first set, suggest that you and your present partner each take on one of the good players as a partner for the remainder of the day.

We have now covered, in both the absolute and the relativistic sense, the principal elements of play that should furnish the foundation for happier incompetence in tennis. It is worth emphasizing, as a final word, that our goal has not been to shift the reader from his basic ability to a higher one. What we have been after is cutting down the errors around which ordinary tennis is built—your errors, that is. It is true that, if you take seriously all we have said, you will appear to be more competent to the other three players on the court. But that will be only because they have fewer occasions than they used to have to register negative impressions of your play.

Your friends will not observe that you send forth lightning-like shots very much more often than you ever used to. But you will be making more points, winning more often. They will still be ordinary, and you will be ex-ordinary. You will be happier and they will be sadder. And you will know why.